CORNISH
FOLK TALES
OF PLACE

CORNISH
FOLK TALES
OF PLACE

TRADITIONAL STORIES FROM
NORTH AND EAST CORNWALL

ANNA CHORLTON

The
History
Press

First published 2019

The History Press
The Mill, Brimscombe Port
Stroud, Gloucestershire, GL5 2QG
www.thehistorypress.co.uk

© Anna Chorlton & Mazed Tales, 2019
Illustrations © individual illustrators, 2019

The right of Anna Chorlton & Mazed Tales to be identified
as the Authors of this work has been asserted in accordance
with the Copyright, Designs and Patents Act 1988.

British Library Cataloguing in Publication Data.
A catalogue record for this book is available from the British Library.

ISBN 978 0 7509 8757 8

Typesetting and origination by The History Press
Printed and bound in Great Britain by TJ International Ltd.

When I was a young child, in the woods behind our house in East Anglia, there was a ditch. It only had water in it during the wettest of winter months. For most of the year it was a deep, dry depression that ran into the heart of the dark wood. My grandfather told me it was the path that the black dog used when out hunting.

I never crossed that ditch.

Granddad has been dead many years. I moved to Cornwall. The story of the dog and the ditch has vanished. In Cornwall I have been introduced to many other stories, such as the ones in this collection, that could easily have disappeared the same way.

Walking on Bodmin Moor in the mist, I've even met some of the characters featured …

You don't have to believe in magic – but it helps!

Mark Camp
Visit Cornwall

CONTENTS

TALES FROM EAST CORNWALL'S RIVERS

TALES FROM BODMIN MOOR

TOWNS ON THE EDGE OF THE MOOR

BODMIN AND BEYOND

TALES FROM NORTH CORNWALL'S MOORS

TALES FROM NORTH CORNWALL'S COAST

ACKNOWLEDGEMENTS

I would like to thank the droll tellers and folk tale collectors who have told and retold, collected and nurtured the folk tales of Cornwall. Without the tradition of droll tellers, travelling and telling tales along the hearth sides of Cornish homes, the tales would be lost as winter leaves. Thanks also go to Sue Field for creating Monochrome Mazed and Mazed Tales on which *Cornish Folk Tales of Place* is based, and who collected the Mazed Tales: her research, inspiration and ideas have been invaluable. Many thanks to Nicola Guy, Local Commissioning Editor at The History Press, for her guidance and for making *Cornish Folk Tales of Place* possible. Thanks also to Ronald M. James for writing the foreword, and to Mark Camp for his story. Many thanks to the Heritage Lottery Fund and Feast Cornwall for funding Mazed and Mazed North digital collections of folk tales of place. Thank you to Denzil Monk for his creativity in producing the animations for Mazed, to Awen's Nick Harpley for the Mazed website, and to all those who took part in Mazed.

A big thank you to everyone who took part in Monochrome Mazed and illustrated *Cornish Folk Tales of Place* so beautifully. Many thanks to the funders for Monochrome Mazed: Feast Cornwall and The History Press. Many thanks to John Roberts of PuppetCraft for the beautiful puppets of Bill and Nellie and for illustrating the Caradoc ballads. Thanks also go to artists Stephen Lambert, Mark Gregory, Keith Sparrow, Alex Goodman and Sophie Fordham for allowing their illustrations from Mazed North to be used in *Cornish Folk Tales of Place*; and to Katherine

Soutar for the front cover illustration. Many thanks to Alicia
Breakspear for the author photograph.

My thanks to Liz Berg, Beta Reader, and to the Society for
Storytelling Gathering in Plymouth organized by Liz, where
the idea for this book began. Many thanks also to the folklore
collectors Enys Tregarthen and Robert Hunt, and to Barbara
Spooner for *Betsy Laundry*: her story collecting remains as
fragments in the journals of the Old Cornwall Society. Many
thanks to Simon Young for his advice, and to Robert Keys for
*Finnygook, Dando and his Dogs, Lady Mount Edgcumbe's Ring,
Patten Peg. Blackberry Round* and *King of the Cormorants*. These
are his stories, told to him as a child and through generations
of his family living around the Rame Peninsula. They can be
found in the Institute of Cornish Studies book, *Memory Place
and Identity*, 2012 Frances Boutle publishers. Many thanks to
John Buckingham and friends for taking the time to talk about
Padstow past and present. And finally, thank you to Dougie
Cummings for his family tale, *A Ghostly Feast at Bethany*.

ILLUSTRATIONS

Monochrome Mazed (part of Mazed Tales) was a lovely community arts project giving people the opportunity to be involved in illustrating their own traditional tales. It brought artists and a storyteller into schools, libraries and a community centre to illustrate the tales of *Cornish Folk Tales of Place* during the summer of 2018.

Three schools took part in Monochrome Mazed. A storyteller visited the schools and told a selection of Mazed Tales to the children, who were then familiar with the stories and characters they were to illustrate. Artists taught illustration techniques to pupils. All the children involved did a fantastic job of illustrating the tales in this book.

Mark Gregory (markgregoryart.weebly.com) ran pen and ink drawing workshops at Launceston Library and Egloskerry Primary School (Year Six, witch tales).

Sue Field (www.mazedtales.org) told the stories at all of the sessions. She worked with silhouettes at Bodmin Library to capture piskey mischief and at Looe Primary Academy potato printing piskeys with Year One and silhouetting saints and smugglers with Year Five.

Keith Sparrow (www.kaspar.co.uk) taught Manga illustration to Year Five at Dobwalls Community Primary School.

Sophie Fordham (www.sophiefordham.co.uk) led an Intaglio printmaking workshop at Liskerrett Community Centre in Liskeard, producing illustrations of the birds and animals found in the tales.

Exciting pictures and prints from all the workshops were displayed on banners in Looe Library, Launceston Library and Liskerrett Community Centre over the summer holidays 2018.

The Monochrome Mazed artists have all contributed illustrations to the book, as have other artists from Mazed and Mazed North.

John Roberts (www.puppetcraft.co.uk) illustrated the Caradoc ballads.

Stephen Lambert illustrated 'The Piskeys Revenge'.

Alex Goodman (www.hope-anchor.co.uk) illustrated Mother Ivey.

The cover illustration is by Katherine Soutar (katherinesoutarillustration.com), cover illustrator for The History Press's Folk Tales series.

PREFACE

The folklore of Cornwall should not be underestimated. Nineteenth-century Cornish folk tales and legends rival those of Celtic cousins in Wales and Scotland, and its publications outdistance those of each English county. Collectors including Robert Hunt, William Bottrell, Nellie Sloggett (writing as Enys Tregarthen) and the father–son team of Jonathan and Thomas Quiller Couch produced books that record traditions to make Cornwall proud. These authors documented a legacy that this volume celebrates.

It would be easy to stop with that point, namely that books preserve an astounding amount of Cornish folklore, but the story does not end there. The publications of collectors and writers would not have been possible had it not been for the storytellers, known in Cornwall as droll tellers. These masterful entertainers took narratives they heard and, in a jovial way, they manipulated them and made them their own. The droll tellers embraced tales from a forgotten time and passed them on to folklorists just as the era of the storyteller seemed to be fading. The droll tellers and their collectors allow the Cornish of today to enjoy a superb cultural inheritance.

With this book, however, Anna Chorlton and Mazed Tales ask us to move beyond cherished publications from previous centuries to resist allowing old narratives to linger as fossilised heirlooms. *Cornish Folk Tales of Place* explores ways that these stories can remain alive, to act as vibrant signposts of what it means to be Cornish. Through retellings and with enchanting illustrations, Anna and a range of artists demonstrate that the age of the droll tellers need never end. This spectrum of talent challenges the reader, challenges all of us to grab the baton and to be our own droll tellers. *Cornish Folk Tales of Place* hints at how each of us can explore the possibilities; how we can all be droll tellers; how we can all be artists.

Ronald M. James
October 2018
Author of *The Folklore of Cornwall: The Oral History of a Celtic Nation* (2018)

INTRODUCTION

Cornish tales are linked to her beautiful and varied landscape. Along the coasts can be found tales of mermaids, witches and smugglers. Along the cliffs are tales of the Cornish fairy folk known as piskeys. Tiny beings, piskeys wear colourful hats and jackets or dresses and often riding breeches. The character of the piskey folk is changeable. They can be helpful and work hard on farms in the day and in homes at night, bringing with them a friendly blessing. If a human interferes in their work, piskeys become mischievous and relish playing tricks. When someone

is led astray on their journey by the piskeys, it is said they have been 'mazed' (confused) by them and 'piskey led'. Piskeys love to dance and sing in the fields and woods of the Cornish countryside. Piskeys ride horses across the moors and take little lanterns along the marshlands. The Cornish moors are also home to tales of great giants and beasts.

At firesides, Cornish tales were traditionally told by droll tellers; wandering storytellers who travelled from place to place, telling tales for supper and a bed for the night.

There are many collections of the tales of West Cornwall; the giants of St Michael's Mount and the Mermaid of Zennor have become widely known. This collection of tales of East Cornwall seeks to redress the balance.

Mazed Tales (www.mazedtales.org) is a successful community arts project collecting the stories of East Cornwall on which *Cornish Folk Tales of Place* is based. Mazed Tales presents the folk tales of East Cornwall on a website of tales, each connected with beautiful photographs of the places they are set in. A geolocational app showed fantastic short animations of twelve of the tales: these can now be viewed on the website and Cornish language (Kernewek) versions are also available. Cornishibai is Mazed's version of Japanese street storytelling using a bike and illustrations of Cornish folk tales to tell the stories. This book is a collection of Mazed Tales and some new tales, with an introduction to each of the places in which the tales are set. Each chapter begins with an old Cornish saying. *Cornish Folk Tales of Place* is illustrated by Mazed artists and the community of East Cornwall.

TALES
FROM EAST
CORNWALL'S
COAST

1

POLPERRO

Piskey fine
Piskey gay
Piskey then will fly away.

Polperro's tales are of piskeys. Polperro is a pretty and ancient fishing village. At the entrance to Polperro is Crumplehorn Inn, the place where the smugglers' banker Zephaniah Job lived and issued his own banknotes. The River Pol runs alongside the road with many stone bridges crossing it. An icy wind blows in from the sea. Farmland and wooded hills edge Polperro on both sides of a long, narrow valley, providing plenty of shelter for piskeys and smugglers alike. Walking or driving through Polperro, visitors have a job not to be piskey led. The lanes are very narrow and delivery vans get stuck: one woman brings wood to her cottage using a quad bike; one lane is a dead end leading directly into the river; a house is propped up by stilts. The houses rise out of the river and surround the harbour: it is almost as if the buildings were floating. A small hole in the harbour wall is the gateway to the sea. The village and the sea live in very close proximity. Fishermen come out of their houses and down steps into their boats. Fisherman John would definitely have been able to hear the piskeys making mischief from his house on the harbour. The past doesn't feel very far away: the tale of 'The Fisherman and the Piskeys' could happen again tonight.

The Fisherman and the Piskeys

A fisherman called John was having a rare night at home in bed instead of out at sea, when there was a shout outside his window. Thinking it was a call to go and secure his boat, John got up and walked the few steps to the harbour. It was a calm night; no gale to be heard, nothing but a faint chattering. The tide was out, his boat was beached and sitting in a ring around it were a group of piskeys.

The piskeys threw their caps into the ring. A piskey with a large sack began dealing out gold pieces. Not one to miss an opportunity, John jumped down onto the sand and slipped his own cap into the ring. When it was more or less full, he snuck his cap out again and started for home. Hearing a shout, John looked back and saw chasing after him a crowd of piskeys. He ran up the steps to his door being closely pursued. Just in time, John closed the door behind him and stuffed a gold piece into the keyhole. He could hear the angry piskeys outside. Now John knew the tales of piskey gold; he knew it always turned from heavy gold coins to bags of leaf and dust in human hands. Making sure the keyhole was properly sealed, John left his cap on the table and climbed the stone stairs to his bed.

In the morning, he woke later than usual and ran down to the kitchen to make a quick breakfast. He kept shaking his head and muttering to himself. What curious dreams he'd been having all night. Piskeys indeed. A fisherman has much greater adversaries in the arms of the sea. John knew he would never have been

bothered by a few pesky piskeys on land. Clearing the table, he found his cap from the night before. John looked inside his cap and to his surprise it was still filled with piskey gold.

COLMAN GREY

A large car park stands at the top of Polperro – once it was fields, where a kind farmer lived.

A farmer was walking home across the fields when he met a very, very small person sitting on a stone. The farmer felt suddenly sorry for the little person because it was huddled up looking cold and miserable. On an impulse, the farmer whisked it up into his pocket and headed on for home. Inside the farmhouse kitchen, the farmer's wife took off the little person's wet clothes and wrapped it in a blanket. She gave it some milk and hoped it would feel happier. And happier it was; the little person looked around the family and grinned at each and every one of them. Then it sprang to life and began to dance and be merry.

For three days the little person entertained the farmer and his family. It brought a good feeling into the poor and work-weary household and somehow things felt easier than before. Everyone had more energy and went about their tasks more willingly.

On the fourth day a voice called out, 'Colman Grey. Colman Grey. Colman Grey.'

And the little person said, 'My dad has come, I must be gone.'

With that the piskey flew through the keyhole and was gone. The farmer and his family never did see the piskey again but a little of his merry energy stayed with them for the rest of their days.

THE MIDWIFE'S TALE

Polperro's tales were collected in the nineteenth century by Jonathan Couch, a doctor who lived in a house that still overlooks the river today. He helped the local midwife with difficult deliveries.

In a cottage in Polperro village lived a midwife called Beth. Beth was a little lady with curling brown hair. Evening time, she sat by the fire knitting and waiting to see if a family needed her service. One night, there came a knocking at the door. When Beth opened it, she was very surprised to see a tiny man, much smaller than even she.

'I am in need of your service,' said the piskey sternly.

Now Beth was unsure of strangers and she hesitated in her reply.

'You'll have use for this,' said the piskey and he thrust a pouch of gold coins into her hands.

Gold was not to be argued with and Beth gathered her things and closed the door to behind her. The piskey helped Beth up onto his horse. Until a moment ago, the piskey horse had been so small Beth hadn't noticed it was there. The horse held her weight and they galloped away through the village, the woods and the fields until they came to a tiny house. The piskey motioned for Beth to hurry. The house was dark and smelled musty and there was very little furniture. A tiny piskey lady lay crying on some straw. Wasting no time, Beth went to the piskey mother and set about her work. She delivered the baby and took it into the bathroom to give it a bath in some warm, soapy water.

While she was carefully washing the baby, some soapy water flicked into her eye. All at once, Beth saw the interior of the house totally differently: it had warm cheerful furnishings and bright lights. Returning to the living room, Beth was overwhelmed by piskeys in every corner, celebrating the birth of the baby in her arms. Beth passed the baby back to its smiling mother and decided not to let on she could see all the visitors. The piskey father ushered her out of the door and onto the horse and they galloped back over the fields and down the valley to Beth's cottage. On the doorstep, the piskey father said, 'Thank you for saving my wife and child. However, you must never breathe a word about tonight to anyone and you will never see me or my family again.'

Beth said simply, 'Good night,' and went back to her knitting.

Polperro's midwife forgot all about her visit from the piskey, that is until the day of the fair. She was enjoying looking at the stalls and had already picked out some fine red wool, when she saw the piskey father moving between the stalls. At each one he stopped to take something and then moved on to the next without paying. Beth decided to have words with the piskey; after all most of the stalls were collecting for charity. Her voice stern but kind, she approached him and said, 'I can see you taking things from the stalls and I hope you don't mind me saying so but you need to pay.'

'Which eye have you seen me with?' shouted the piskey, running towards her.

'Well this eye I think,' said Beth, pointing to her right eye.

The piskey jumped up and punched Beth in the eye. He ran off without an explanation and Beth lost her piskey sight and all sight in her right eye from that moment to this.

The Devil's Doorway

Some say, long ago, there was an earthquake in Polperro that caused the rock to split. Some say it was the Devil himself. For the Devil lived a time in the slate behind Polperro, hiding there in the day. At night, he would ride out on his great black horse and cart, shrieking as he raced along the wild Cornish coast. The fishing families and the farming families slept through the Devil's games as they were exhausted after a long day's work outside.

One night, the Devil rode out: his eyes were red burning coals, his hands razor-sharp talons, his cloak and hood blacker than night. He stank of rancid caves. His apparition was so frightening the very rock beneath him split in a huge tear. The Devil's horse reared in triumph. As its hooves crashed down, a hoof print was left in the rock, leaving behind a hoof-shaped pool.

2

LOOE

'Jack the giant with nothing to do
built a hedge from Lerryn to Looe.'

Looe is a town of the senses: the smells of pasties, beer, chips, fish and the sea; the sounds of boats, clattering cutlery, conversation; and sights perfect for a photograph. Every alleyway and reflection has something beautiful about it. Every inch of the river, the subtle reach of a calm sea, an invitation to jump in a boat of any description or simply swim. Or on a rough, stormy day, experience the feeling of closeness to nature's savagery while standing in the heart of town. This gives Looe an edgy dimension, an undercurrent to a place whose stories are of smugglers and ghosts.

THE SPECTRAL COACH

Between Polperro and Looe is the village of Talland and this is the tale of a vicar of Talland church, a Reverend Richard Dodge. Reverend Dodge was vicar at Talland between 1713 and 1747 and was well known for being an exorcist. Every night, Dodge went out onto the highway to remonstrate with restless spirits. It was said that on seeing him the spirits screamed, 'Dodge is come, I must be gone,' and disappeared into the night. Some say the exorcisms were a cover for a large smuggling operation he was running from the beach up Bridle Lane to the church, and that's as well may be. This however, is not a tale of smuggling; it is a tale of the laying to rest of the Spectral Coach.

Blackadon Moor, near Lanreath, had always been common land until, that is, the local landowners tried to claim it. An ugly dispute broke out and one of the landowners got so worked up by the failure to resolve the dispute – and divide up the land – he died of a rage. Even in death, he would not give up his claim to the land. He haunted it as a terrible apparition driving a coach pulled by headless horses.

The most direct route to Lanreath village was to cross the common land and it became a regular occurrence for villagers to become mazed, confused of their direction, or even to suffer insanity as a result of an encounter with the Spectral Coach. The well-being of the village was becoming increasingly and adversely affected by the Spectre. One day, the Reverend Parson Mills of Lanreath sent a letter to Reverend Richard Dodge of Talland asking him to lay the Spectre to rest. Dodge arranged to meet Mills one dark night out on the moor.

Dodge and Mills talked long into the night and prayed for the Spectre's soul. When it didn't appear, the two men thought the job must have been done and they went their separate ways. Dodge

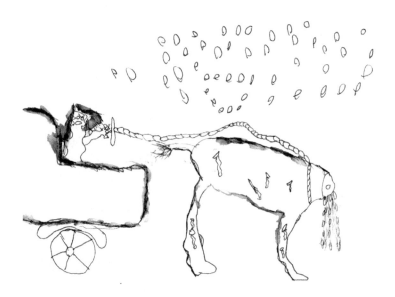

had ridden most of the way back to Talland, when his horse stopped still and refused to go forward. He gave the horse its head and it threw Dodge off and galloped back up to the moor. Dodge ran after it, stumbling along the uneven path. When finally he reached the moor, a terrifying sight played out before him.

Mills lay on the ground at the feet of two steaming, headless horses, a coach and a horrifying Spectre with burning red eyes set within a huge black skull. The Spectre dismounted and walked toward Mills. With all the strength and power within him Dodge began to pray. He prayed with more passion and conviction than ever before, willing his fear to disperse so he could calmly defeat the Spectre. All at once the Spectre turned towards Dodge and for one terrible moment, the brave reverend thought he would be consumed by the anger sweeping from the apparition. Then it shrieked, 'Dodge is come, I must be gone.'

The Spectre climbed back into the coach, he drove away across Blackadon Moor and disappeared.

Those inflicted with insanity immediately felt well and the villagers of Lanreath never saw the angry coachman again.

If you are walking along the cliffs or fields between Talland and Lanreath and you see the Spectral Coach, you know what to say.

'Dodge is come! So, you be gone.'

The White Hare of Looe

Sarah was a serious girl with every good intention. She worked in the harbour, hawking the catch. She had her life planned and made certain she got what she wanted. Simon was a cheerful lad but fickle. He loved Sarah deeply for a year and a day until he changed his mind. Simon decided Sarah was a bit bland, and he started dating Sally, a barmaid at the Jolly Sailor. Now Sarah still loved Simon truly and deeply, and she could not change her opinion. She thought Simon would make a suitable husband and had their life together all mapped out – but it was not to be. Simon now loved Sally. The humiliation of rejection stung and jibbed at poor, serious Sarah's soul. Her pride was hurt and her spirit seethed with resentment. When Simon became Sally's husband and not Sarah's, Sarah died of a broken heart. Simon lived together with Sally in a higgledy-built house in West Looe. Their home was just up from the harbour and a tiny saunter from the *Jolly Sailor* Inn. Now a little of Sarah's anguish lingered after her death and fixated on hurting Simon's happiness. Every night, her ghost bounded down Talland Hill in the form of a white hare and followed Simon into the *Jolly Sailor*. The white hare haunted him with all the force of her humiliation.

One night, on her way down the hill, the white hare spotted a storm brewing out at sea. Many a member of Sarah's family would be heading out in their boats and Sarah had to warn them. From that night on whenever she sensed a storm, Sarah took to bounding between the ropes tying the boats along the harbour. It became common for the people of Looe to see a large white hare running between the boats. The town people came to recognise the helpful hare was trying to warn of a storm and save the lives of the men of Looe. And though she was very relieved at the success of her new ghostly task, the bitterness kept Sarah appearing on her nightly mission and she always doubled back to find Simon, the man who had betrayed her. Not being a very strong character himself, Simon was soon overcome by the taunts of the white hare and its constant reminder of his jilting of serious Sarah. There was nothing jolly Sally could do to calm his regret, for the hare was always there to remind them. Within the year, Simon too died of ill health and the ghost of the hare stood ready to claim him. Sometimes still the white hare is spotted on West Looe Hill – sign of another fickle lad, sign of another broken-hearted maid, sign of a fierce storm brewing.

THE COCK-CROW STONE

The swell was fine as the tide pushed in between the Banjo Pier and along the harbour wall over Saunders Lane. Here a great pile of white rock once hoisted above the water. The white rock struck a pose as a gleaming landmark fronting Looe Harbour.

Every day a cock was heard to crow with urgent persistence. His message vibrated through the stones. Sensitive as well as splendid, the pile of white rocks felt the cockerel bragging and knew the hour when the day's eggs were to be laid.

The tide pushed in and the rocks swelled with their own response to the bird's exaltation. With a slow majesty the top rock turned three full circles, nodding its crest to the crow of Hay Farm.

Joseph of Arimathea brings Jesus to Looe by Boat

Looe Island was a good landing place for smugglers and in the 1780s it was home to smuggler brother and sister, Amram and Jochabed Hooper. The Hoopers smuggled goods from Guernsey and Roscoff and held them on Looe Island until it was safe to bring them in to Looe. Looe Island is also said to be the place Jesus stayed when visiting Cornwall with his uncle Joseph of Arimathea.

Joseph of Arimathea was a seafaring merchant who traded saffron for tin. One day he set out with a group of people he had invited to join him. One of his companions was his nephew, Jesus of Nazareth. They came at last to Brittany and here Joseph left his passengers to spend some months exploring the landscape. Taking with him only young Jesus, Joseph sailed for Cornwall. When they were in sight of land, Jesus spotted an island and they anchored beside it. Joseph left Jesus playing on the beach while he rowed a little dinghy the short distance to Looe.

Looe was bustling with traders. Tin was mined on the moors and brought down to Looe on pack horses. Joseph knew Looe was the best place for him to trade saffron for tin. The Cornish were shrewd and sharp-witted traders and Joseph would have to have his wits about him. He was tired after the long day sailing but knew he had something the other tin traders didn't. Saffron was very special in Cornwall; the people used the golden spice to

bake buns and bread, and the Looe men were happy to trade their tin for Joseph's saffron. Filling the dinghy with tin, Joseph rowed back to the island. Joseph found Jesus still happily playing.

'Come Jesus, we have been invited to a tinner's supper.'

Jesus helped Joseph unload the tin from the dinghy and secure it safely on the sailing boat. They anchored just off Looe and paddled ashore. On the beach a merry crowd gathered around a good fire. Fish were cooked on large flat stones and a meal was eaten by all. The tinners talked mostly of wolfram, a substance that rose when they smelted the tin and devoured the tin like a wolf. The men complained about losing their tin. Joseph told them a secret of how to rid the tin of the wolfram. The men of Looe were very grateful and told him he would always be welcome in the busy seaside town.

On a journey to Glastonbury, Joseph planted his staff, which grew to be the Glastonbury thorn tree. An abbey was founded at Glastonbury and in time, the monks retraced Joseph's steps back to Looe Island and built a chapel there. Later, the monks moved the chapel to Lammana at Hannafore, where some stones still remain.

Most people think the saints brought Christianity to Cornwall but the people of Looe know better.

AMRAM AND JOCHABED

It was a grey stormy day and the excise men were known to be on their way to Plymouth. Amram watched their boat sail around the headland before beginning the task of rolling smuggled barrels out of the farmhouse door on Looe Island and down to his boat on little beach. His sister, Jochabed, carried armfuls of silks, tea and tobacco: all was to be loaded and taken to Looe. At last the boat was full and they set off rowing across the bay. It wasn't far to Looe but halfway across, out of the corner of his eye, Amram saw what looked to be another excise boat approaching the island from Fowey. It was heading straight for Looe and if it didn't catch up with them on the way, it would surely reach Looe just as Amram fixed his boat up at West Looe. A crowd waited to help him empty the load. There was nothing for it: with a heavy heart, Amram began heaving the contraband goods into the sea. Perhaps he would retrieve them when the tide was low; most likely he wouldn't. He continued on to Looe and took himself for a sorry pint in the *Jolly Sailor*. Amram told whoever would listen of his lost load.

'Every time I try to take my contraband goods across to Looe from the island, the excise men are there waiting. I've lost a good load today but I've a lot more to shift off the island before I go to sea to fetch any more.'

The landlady, who had been listening intently, took him aside.

'You have been using my pub to store smuggled goods for some time now and I trust you enough to let you into my greatest secret.'

'You do?'

'From this pub runs a secret passage all the way to Looe Island. Keep me in the finest silks and my pub in the very best brandy and you can use it whenever you like.'

Amram was soon on his way, rowing back to Looe Island to tell Jochabed of his fantastic discovery. The *Jolly Sailor's* landlady had told him where to find the entrance to the tunnel from the island. That very night, the brother and sister would set out on their first of many trips. Amram and Jochabed would carry the contraband along the damp tunnel from the island to the *Jolly Sailor*, with no fear of the excise men ever catching sight of them.

3

SEATON TO RAME

'Pilchards are food, money and light
All in one night.'

*Along the coast from Seaton to Rame Head are black ragged rocks
and sandy coves. In winter, with industrial repetition the waves roar
and crash. A bright light hits the sea and the sands. On a fine day the
summer sea is turquoise and mesmerising. Downderry Beach has a
fleet of red-sailed boats and a sensitive mermaid swims in Seaton Bay.
Dando and his dogs run back and forth along the cliff path and in
days gone smugglers worked through the night. The huer stood on the
cliffs, watching the seas for signs of a shoal of pilchards swelling the
bays. When the huer saw the pilchards, he would shout to the fishermen who would set out in groups of three boats to trap the fish in a
wide net called a seine.*

THE SEATON MERMAID

Once Seaton was a prosperous port with crowds of people working on the quay. The grand harbour wall was built in an arc shielding an impressive fleet of boats. On either side of the river many houses nestled on the hills. The port was full of traders and activity. Out in the bay a mermaid played, her hair shimmered gold then green. A shoal of pilchards swam all about her. A great silver tail appeared and disappeared as she dived through the waves.

A crowd gathered on the cliffs, excited to see the pilchards within easy reach. The huer's shout went out and the whole town watched as the first three boats launched. Sailing a smaller lurcher boat was Paul Pengelly, a well-liked young man with sandy hair. The mermaid surfaced right by his boat and he couldn't help smiling down at her. The mermaid smiled back. She was pretty as pilchards and Paul was instantly smitten. She gestured for Paul to come and play with her and she swam easily in the sunlit sea. But Paul had a job to do and he signalled for the seine to form, and a curved line of net flanked the shoal. The sound of pilchards thwacking their tails was all Paul could hear to begin with and then, building from beneath the familiar beat came another sound; the sound of the mermaid screaming with rage.

Too late, Paul tried to free the mermaid from his nets. He knew he should have warned her and waited until she had finished playing her game. At last he disentangled her and freed her into the waves. As she turned to look back, the mermaid had no smile for Paul Pengelly.

'I curse you and all of Seaton,' she shouted, her whole body seething with fury.

Paul knew there was worse to come and soon. He tried to turn the boat back to the safety of the harbour but again he was too late. Paul watched helplessly as the mermaid conjured a sand-storm. The sand fell in huge swathes covering the harbour and buildings, burying the port of Seaton forever.

Nowadays, Seaton is a pretty beach and village with a nature reserve and walk along the river valley. The mermaid continues to shift the sands; the river rarely meets the sea in the same place and recently the beach cafe was almost destroyed by a storm and covered in sands. The cafe was soon rebuilt, unlike the harbour wall and port, which never recovered. Instead, the port of Plymouth took increasing prominence along the coast and is to this day the prosperous port, just as Seaton once was before Paul Pengelly incurred the wrath of the Seaton Mermaid.

A Voyage with the Piskeys

Porthallow is a hamlet near Talland Bay with a few scattered farm-houses and a green. One day a young farmhand was sent off on an errand to Polperro to the shop. He was running along on his way back when he heard a voice saying, 'I am for Porthallow Green.'

The young man stopped and enjoying a bit of banter, he echoed, 'I am for Porthallow Green,' wishing he was there already. And he found himself on Porthallow Green surrounded by little laughing piskeys.

After a few moments a cry was heard, 'I am for Seaton Beach.'

Thinking this was fun the lad repeated, 'I am for Seaton Beach.' In an instant he found himself on Seaton Beach. He put his errand down and joined a ring of piskeys dancing on the sand.

Then the cry came again, 'I am for the King of France's Cellar.'

Hopefully, the lad repeated, 'I am for the King of France's Cellar.' He found himself being poured a drink of the finest wine in the King of France's very best cellar.

He explored his new surroundings in astonishment for he had never been far from his village. This was a splendid building with a fine table laid out for a feast. Thinking he would like a souvenir of some sort, he quickly pocketed a golden goblet from the table before the cry came again, 'I am for Seaton Beach.'

The lad repeated it, 'I am for Seaton Beach,' not particularly wanting to be left in a foreign land forever, rich as it was.

Reaching the beach, he was just in time to retrieve his parcel from the tide when the cry came, 'I am for Porthallow Green,' and the lad said, 'I am for Porthallow Green.' He was soon back in Porthallow.

That night he told his family about his adventure. They looked at one another and said, 'The lad is mazed.' And the lad, knowing they would have thought this, pulled a shining treasure from his pocket. The farmhand's family examined the golden goblet belonging to the King of France in amazement and it stayed in the family for generations.

FINNYGOOK

The cliffs around Portwrinkle and Crafthole are haunted by the ghost of Silas Finn, or 'Finny' as he was fondly known. In Finny's day, two cargoes were landed at Portwrinkle and along Whitsand Bay; one from the sea and one from France. Finny landed contraband onto the beach at Portwrinkle, the small cove below the village now known as Finnygook Beach. At high tide Finnygook Beach is shielded by the cliffs; from the village you can see only the sea. Finnygook Beach was the perfect place for smugglers' boats to come in. The excise men were rarely local and didn't know the coast as well as they should. Added to the location, Portwrinkle had a thriving and legitimate pilchard business, with many fish cellars nestled in the cliffs. Fishermen loaded baskets of pilchards onto donkeys at Finnygook Beach and took them up the cliffs to Portwrinkle along Donkey Lane. This process also took place along the cliffs past Tregantle at Whitsand Bay. Here, a second Donkey Lane led all the way to Millbrook. When the baskets were empty of pilchards, the smugglers, led by Finny, loaded the donkeys with a second cargo and sent them up the cliffs. No one gave them a second glance. Once at Millbrook, the donkeys stopped at the Highland House where the loot was stowed. Millbrook wives were never short of tea, brandy and sumptuous silks to twirl in. When the route to the river was clear, the smuggled goods were taken across the Tamar to Plymouth. Finny organised all the smuggling from Looe, Lammana, Crafthole, Causland and all the way to the Mewstone in Wembury Bay in Devon.

A popular local man, Finny would do anything for anyone. He enjoyed the thrill of the secret trade. While he was out conducting business, Finny wore a woman's bonnet called a gook as a disguise. A gook was a bal maiden's bonnet and had a very wide brim to keep the rock dust off the face, making it an especially good disguise. Wearing the bonnet, Finny walked about arm in arm with a woman named Black Joan. Some thought Joan was his wife, others thought her a business companion as she was herself a successful smuggler based at Lammana and Looe.

One night, Finny was down on the beach unloading a boat heavy with contraband when he was caught. He had a good lot of brandy unloaded and there was no denying his involvement and no escape. Finny was facing an almost definite hanging. It was on that night, on Finnygook Beach, Finny struck a deal.

Some nights later, Finny stood waving a lantern on the cliff above the beach as the smugglers' boat came by. They knew Finny's lantern as a sign the beach was clear and it was safe to land. A cargo of tea, lace, brandy and tobacco was landed. The smugglers were very surprised when they realised Finny had lured them into a trap. Excise men sprang out at them and took Finn's friends into custody. Amongst them were Amram Hooper and his sister Jochabed. When the smugglers were all caught, Finny fled saving only himself.

In Looe Guildhall hangs a painting, *Arrest of the Smuggler*. It has Amram Hooper and Jochabed in the foreground and in the background is a dark figure watching the arrest who could very possibly be Joan. The beach at Portwrinkle is still called Finnygook Beach after Finny and his bonnet and the inn at Crafthole is Finnygook Inn. Finny never forgave himself for betraying his friends and his restless spirit haunts the cliffs as he searches for a chance to make amends. Perhaps one dark night you might see the smuggler's ghost haunting the cliffs yourself.

TALES
FROM EAST
CORNWALL'S
RIVERS

4

THE RIVER LYNHER

'The devil is afraid to come to Cornwall,
for fear of being baked in a pie.'

*Travelling through Rame Peninsula there is a feeling of proximity to
water, the rivers Lynher and Tamar and the constant smell of the sea.
The English Channel lies to the south and Plymouth Sound to the
east: the River Lynher is north-west and the merging Tamar Estuary
to the north-east. Water characterises the friendly villages and towns
on the banks of the Lynher. Stories are still told in the River Lynher's
valleys: tales in this chapter were collected by the Institute of Cornish
Studies and by the Mazed project. These tales are full of encounters
with animals, fish and birds.*

*The Edgcumbe family owned a lot of land; they had two deer
parks, one spanning the Rame Peninsula and one at Stonehouse.
They built a great house in their deer park at Rame and in 1537 the
Edgcumbe family moved from Cotehele to Mount Edgcumbe House
and made it their main residence. Lord Edgcumbe's house was a fairy
tale palace with its walls rendered white. Sadly, it was bombed in the
Second World War and the interior was destroyed by fire, as was the
entire west wing. The house wasn't rebuilt until a government grant
was secured in the 1950s for a more modest but still handsome castle.
St Julian's Well is the oldest building in the park, dating back to the
fourteenth or fifteenth century. A spring feeds a cistern in its chapel.*

LADY MOUNT EDGCUMBE'S RING

Maker Church was beautifully decorated ready for the wedding of Lord Mount Edgcumbe and his bride-to-be. They were to be married the next morning and thought they would like to take the walk up through the wooded deer park to the church on the hill. The young couple visited the church and then walked the short distance along a small path to St Julian's Well. On the way down the hill, they were talking happily about the day to come, when the bride-to-be slipped and immediately fell into a trance. On instinct, the lord went to the well and dipped his cup into

the well water. He looked about him; the River Lynher was silent as the trees. Lord Mount Edgcumbe held the well water for his bride-to-be to drink. He held his breath and as the water passed the young lady's lips, she was revived.

The next day they were married and returned to Mount Edgcumbe House for a great feasting and dancing. Late that night they retired to their rooms and exhausted, the bride fell into a trance. Lord Mount Edgcumbe sent a lady's maid to St Julian's Well for a cup of its spring water. Again, the water touched the lady's lips and again she was revived.

The newlyweds were very happy together and soon found they were expecting a baby. They spent a lot of time walking by the river. A golden light gave the trees a warm glow. All was quiet and still except for a cormorant bobbing on the river. Those first months were heavenly for Lord and Lady Mount Edgcumbe and it seemed nothing could spoil their happiness, until one day, Lady Mount Edgcumbe was found in a death-like trance. No breath passed her lips; her body was lifeless. The lady's maid was nowhere to be found so Lord Mount Edgcumbe sent his manservant Tanner to St Julian's Well. Tanner went to the kitchens to collect a pitcher and set out in the direction of the well. The well was a long walk away and Tanner did not see why the lady needed well water in particular; it all sounded like a lot of nonsense to him. Passing the pigsties, Tanner dipped the pitcher into their water trough and ambled back to the house. Again, Lord Mount Edgcumbe brought the pitcher to his lady's lips but to his surprise, this time it failed to revive her. Lady Mount Edgcumbe was quite dead.

Lady Mount Edgcumbe was buried in the family vault in her prettiest dress, wearing all her wedding jewels. That night, when the family had retired to bed, Tanner was sitting in the kitchens with an ale, when he began to think about the diamond ring on the lady's wedding finger. He crept back to the vault, and in the light of his lantern, he saw the diamond flash. Tanner took out his saw and took the lady's finger in his. With a deep breath, he began to saw. A horrific scream filled the vault. Lady Mount Edgcumbe was revived from her trance.

Lord and Lady Mount Edgcumbe became closer than ever, walking every day arm in arm by the river. Their baby was born safe and well but Lord Mount Edgcumbe never did find his man-servant to thank him.

PATTEN PEG

Patten Peg lived up Antony, a village overlooking the River Lynher. Peg tapped about in wooden overshoes called pattens, worn to keep the mud off her feet. Antony was very wet and muddy in those days. On muddy days the mud went squelch in her pattens and on a dry day they went tap tap on the road. Whatever the weather, you could always hear Peg coming. Patten Peg was very poor and in need of a little charity but she had a vile temper and a habit of getting angry with all she met. One day, Peg asked her neighbour for some milk and he refused. The neighbour said if she wanted milk she should treat people with kindness. This threw Peg into a violent rage and she cursed him. Again, the neighbour said Patten Peg should be kinder as curses didn't generally encourage folks to give gifts. Patten Peg just laughed at him and disappeared into her cottage.

Not long after their encounter, the neighbour died. Time passed and one day, Patten Peg went to the graveyard, tap tap tappity tap up the many stone steps to the neighbour's grave.

Here, under the shroud of night, Peg dug him up. Waving her lantern frantically over the grave, she located his leg. Peg took the leg home with her and used it to make a stew.

The following night, Peg was feeling terribly lonely. It was bitterly cold in her cottage and she had nothing but bones on her table. Peg began thinking about her neighbour and his advice and decided to concoct a spell to make herself kinder. She ground up the thigh bones to mix with spiders to make her spell. But the spell was too strong and Patten Peg fell mortally ill. On her death her ghost roamed the churchyard looking for her neighbour's grave.

She can still be heard now as her footsteps patter on the church steps at Antony. Peg waits for her neighbour's spirit to tell him how sorry she is and show him kinder ways.

The Witch and the Toad

Another elderly woman from Antony was known as Aunt Alsey. She also had a violent temper and many said she was a witch. Aunt Alsey's landlord was called John Richards. John lived across the Tamar in Devonport, then known as Dock. He would cross the Tamar on a regular basis to collect his rent. Aunt Alsey never paid rent; she had lived in the cottage for as long as anyone could remember and considered it her own. Richards had decided enough was enough with Alsey; he needed the rent to make repairs on the cottages. One day there was a disagreeable scene between Alsey and Richards. Alsey flew into a violent rage and cursed Richard's wife and unborn child. Richards wisely retreated, planning to return another day.

Richards lived at the back of a grocery shop. His wife served customers while he sat at the kitchen table doing the ordering and accounts. One day a toad fell onto the scales while Mrs Richards was busy weighing onions. The toad fell heavily, squashing Mrs Richard's arm and in the shock of it, Mrs Richards fainted. Mr Richards tried to revive her and when he couldn't, in his

frustration he took the hot tongs from the fire, picked up the toad and threw it out of the window.

Next morning, feeling remorse at his action toward the toad, Mr Richards went outside to bury it. But the toad was nowhere to be seen. He went back into the kitchen to order some more vegetables. That afternoon a customer was in the shop telling a story of a woman known as Aunt Alsey who had died the previous night in a fire; her body had been found branded by a pair of tongs. Richards thought he knew exactly how this had come to pass and, considering the curse she had cast on him, felt fearful for his wife and unborn child. The child was born healthily however and grew up a strong lad who later joined the navy. His parents were immensely proud of his memory as his ship was lost. The lad, who could cope with anything on land, was helpless amongst the stormy waves and died at sea.

BLACKBERRY ROUND

Walking through the fields between Antony and St John you might hear a howling of a great black dog in the night. This is a tale of that creature.

Miller Mathews worked a successful mill at St John. By late afternoon on every day of the week, Miller Mathews had twenty bags of flour stacked in sacks. When he was done, he hung a heavy iron bar across the door of the mill and left the flour sacks for the warmth of the family kitchen. The mill family were very loving; Miller Mathew's wife hugged him close as he came in from work and his children played happily all about them.

It happened on three consecutive full moons. On the first full moon, three old ladies came into the yard, changed into toads

and walked off with three sacks of flour on their backs. Miller Mathews couldn't work out how they carried the flour. The disappearance of Miller Mathew's flour was a mystery indeed.

On the second full moon, Mathews hid in a thicket close to the mill and watched. Out of nowhere, three old ladies arrived in his yard, changed into toads and crawled under the jagged edge of the mill door. The tiny toads came out carrying five bags of flour between them. Miller Mathews was about to come out of hiding and accost them, when three huge black dogs with fiery red eyes ran into the yard and took the sacks. The dogs ran off into the night howling. Miller Mathews followed the dogs over the fields. They ran into the blackberry round and disappeared, taking the sacks of flour into the bramble thicket. Miller Mathews turned back for home and to bed, too surprised to follow them.

On the third full moon, Miller Mathews left his family at home, and went outside armed with several guns. As before, he went to the thicket to watch. The sequence of events was almost the same; the three ladies arrived in the yard, they turned into toads and took nine bags of flour from the mill. Out of nowhere three black dogs appeared and took the flour off into the night. This time Miller Mathews followed them across the fields. He hesitated as they dived into the blackberry round and then he dived in after them. Miller Mathews thought he could take back the flour loaded up beneath the round.

Finding nothing there, Miller Mathews ran back home. His family stood in the yard waiting for him, for some reason they were standing with guns raised. He tried to run into his wife's arms so she could hug him close but at that moment she shot him dead. He lay in the yard, a huge ragged mound of black fur with dying fiery eyes.

Blackberry Round was magic, and a dive into its tangles on a full moon had turned the Miller into a black dog, black as flour weevils, black as blackberries. So, I'd steer clear of the Blackberry Round on a full moon if I were you.

DANDO AND HIS DOGS

From the hamlet of Sheviock, St George's Lane leads through woodland down to the River Lynher. Years ago, cattle were driven across the river from Erth Barton at low tide and up St George's Lane and sold at the chartered market at Crafthole. St George's Lane is also the place where the Devil gathered all the lost souls of the parish and drove them down the lane into the Dandy Hole. The Dandy Hole is said to be on Erth Barton side of the river; a great hole leading all the way down to hell.

The priory at St Germans was a place of prayer, ritual and routine. However, one day the prior, who was named John, broke with the Sabbath to go hunting and he persuaded a hunting party to join him. They were fortunate enough to spot a stag and chased after it through the woods. In his enthusiasm, Prior John was separated from the hunt and found himself completely alone, save for his horse and his hounds, in Sheviock Woods. Prior John was unused to being alone when out hunting and he felt a sudden sense of disquiet. Then he saw a huge majestic animal and although he knew his horse was lame, Prior John pushed on and forced the horse to gallop in pursuit. At last he had to stop and rest. Prior John sniffed the air and was sure he could smell meat cooking. Peering through the trees, he could just make out a stranger tending a fire. Screwing up his eyes, John looked again and again until he was sure what he was seeing was real. The stranger had a magnificent feast laid out with meats and wine. 'Come eat with me,' the stranger commanded. And Prior John thought, *Why not?* and went to join him.

The feast was the best he had ever eaten. The stranger's company felt exciting. When he had eaten all he could, Prior John lay back against a tree, his hunting dogs gathering around him. 'I would go to hell and back to find such good food again,' he said.

'So you shall,' said the stranger. And in a moment his appearance changed. He stood up straight and strong, horns grew from his head. He called Prior John's dogs to heel and a great black horse appeared from the shadows. Prior John knew the only thing he could do was to run to his horse and make his escape. The stag had evaded him; perhaps he could do the same and escape the Horned Hunter. A second chase began and Dando, the Horned Hunter, chased Prior John with his own hounds. He chased him through the parishes, along the cliffs from Downderry to Portwrinkle, all the way to Rame and back again to Sheviock.

Prior John hoped he would be returned to St Germans but he was chased on down St George's Lane. The lane was steep, leading on down to the river. He looked at the familiar fields and woodland where he had first seen the stag and wished he had chosen to stay with his hunting party and do things differently. He longed to pray by the River Tiddy on the mud flats. Perhaps if he prayed, the Horned Hunter would disappear, cowed by the love of the Lord. Prior John knelt to pray but the Horned Hunter just laughed.

'Your piety comes too late,' he said with menace, watching Prior John as he staggered back to his horse.

St George's Lane was walled with ivy, rain patted into a stream running through leaves and over the stones as the lane narrowed and dove steeply down to the River Lynher. Prior John did not dismount when he got to the river's edge. Instead, his faithless hounds drove him on into the water and down, down the deep Dandy Hole all the way to Hell.

Never again, did anyone at St Germans Priory go hunting on the Sabbath and Prior John was seen no more. Dando and his dogs however, are often seen chasing along the cliffs at night, screaming and howling along with the wind. In St Germans Church can be found a fifteenth-century wood carving of Dando and his Dogs on a misericord seat.

KING OF THE CORMORANTS

Dando and his Dogs is the first of two tales of the fiery fates of those destined for the Dandy Hole. The second concerns Ince Castle, a grade one listed building with a large estate almost surrounded by the waters of the River Lynher: hence the name Ince, from the Cornish word 'enys,' meaning island. It was built in 1642 by Henry Killigrew, diplomat, politician and MP for Looe. Ince Castle is striking in that it has four towers, one built on each corner. The gardens, full of beautiful azaleas, give way to farmland edged by the river. Seen from the castle the Lynher is wide and tree lined, its expansive waters run mud grey. Along the river's edge, the sounds are birdsong, sheep calling their lambs and a rustling of new leaves being blown by the wind. From the back of the house Plymouth can be seen. Standing in the midst of carefully managed scented gardens, it is hard to imagine this was once the haunt of a ruthless bigamist. This is his story.

A large bird with outstretched wings surveys the farmland from his perch on a tree on the banks of the River Lynher. The wind buffers his back and he holds his position with forceful determination as his wings dry and the fish settle. It is a short walk from the rough scrubland of the river's edge to the waving reeds and grasses of the wasteland on the perimeter of Ince's farm. Henry Killigrew strides blithely through the boggy fields and vaults the heavy stone stile into the yard.

Farmer Ince is seated to his second full breakfast, a huge red neckerchief beneath his chin and gravy sauce dripping from his beard. He is surrounded by four girls with the same black hair and cheeks flushed by the heat of the stove. The chill wind chases them as they go about their many chores in the farmyard. Henry bristles at the injustice of this farmer's over-reliance on his daughters. He flaps his arms absently against his sides as he schemes on how best to approach the household.

The door opens quickly and Danielle beckons him in. She smiles at Henry. 'I am to invite you in, Father said. I do hope you haven't come far. You look a bit … wet.' Henry takes her in with his black coal eyes and lifting off his hat, he slips inside as bidden.

'Ah, a stranger in these parts is not often had, especially one walking into my yard on his own without an errand,' says Farmer Ince. He glares at Henry, 'Or have you an errand?'

Henry stands to the side with what he hopes is a gallant wave to one of the girls as a plate is brought before the farmer and a tank of cider.

'Anything for you, sir?' she asks shyly.

'Anything for you, sir,' her father echoes. 'This one is not a sir, not as I am aware of anyways. Am I correct or am I correct?'

'Who knows?' says Henry evasively. 'Yes, I would like a drink. My mouth appears full of salt and I haven't a scrap of ham for breakfast. This must be rich and fruitful lands you have here, with enough luck to produce four equally beautiful if work- and wind-touched daughters.'

'Nothing 'as touched my daughters. You are the first who said my land is profit.'

'Oh yes.' Henry leans toward the farmer, his pointed beard jutting from his chin and his eyes finding and holding Ince's. 'Your land is just what I have been searching for. I would like to buy your land.'

'Since when have I sold any of my land? I never said it was for sale and if it was, you just said yourself, it would fetch a very high price. Who are you anyway?'

'Henry Killigrew to you.' He puts out his hand. Farmer Ince ignores Henry's hand, waving him outside. Ince slowly follows the younger man, they look out over the stone stile and into the boggy wasteland. Ince sniffs the air; it is flat and quiet on the river bank, cormorants hang their wings in the old beech tree. Farmer Ince makes up his mind and demands thirty sacks of silver, thirty sacks of gold and a lease of three lives for the land. Henry looks at him and pulls at his pointy waxy beard.

'I will not accept anything less,' says Farmer Ince nervously, observing this young man standing in his yard without so much as a sack of belongings.

'What is it you have an excess of?' Henry asks him.

'It would not be advisable to mock me, Killigrew.'

'I have only a certain amount of gold but I will take from you a daughter in marriage.'

'I will need the full amount of gold and silver, enough sacks to fill the pigsty and if you can get it to me by the end of the day you can keep the land as long as you remain married to a daughter of mine.' Ince feels pleased: this arrangement would keep the land tied to the farm and not cut off without a tithe or a connection.

Henry stands tall with his legs spaced wide and strokes his beard. Within the time it took to clear the table, the land is sold and Henry strides from the farmyard and over the stile from whence he came. Farmer Ince walks slowly across the yard to the pigsty. An unfamiliar shadow runs across his yard and another up the side of the pigsty and as he looks up, he is puzzled as can be, for a tall black tower appears to have grown out of his old field. As he peers over, he blinks as much as usually helps his vision, but it is still there, as are three sister towers and an extravagant castle to hold them. He shakes his head for there are no windows.

Soon after the castle is built, the wedding is held for Killigrew and Ince's eldest daughter, Danielle. It is a modest affair and she soon leaves to live in the castle. One month later, the strange man with the pointed beard stands once more in Farmer Ince's parlour. He explains the sorry news of the untimely death of Danielle. As part of the bargain he must take another of Ince's daughters for his bride. Now Farmer Ince has always disliked his second daughter, Tegan: she is stout and he resents the share she takes of his meat and cheese. He looks at the man before him, dressed quite rightly from head to toe in black, and nods to Tegan to go take his hand.

A month later, a message arrives informing him that Tegan has also died and demanding the farmer hold to his bargain and hand over his third daughter. The farmer, who is begrudging the fact that he now has to do much of the work around house and farm with two daughters gone, is not so sure he has a good bargain. However, his youngest daughter, Caroline, had always been his favourite and he would like to have her for company – and she does make the best roast dinner. The third daughter climbs the stone stile and is married to the stranger in the castle.

When the message comes that the third daughter has died and Ince is obliged to hand over his youngest and favoured daughter, the farmer loses his apathy and roars with anger. He offers Henry all the gold and silver along with the pig but tells Henry he cannot take Caroline; she will stay on the farm. Henry does not even stand to consider. He appears at the window at dusk, wraps Caroline in a cloak in a pretence at chivalry and takes her to his castle.

At night no light can be seen from outside as the four towers stand another shade within the blackness. Yet inside, four candles burn and the four Ince daughters live unbeknown to one another within the towers of Killigrew's castle. Caroline Ince makes the best of the cramped stone room in which she finds herself. She folds her bedclothes and her shawl and dusts the floor with black feathers she finds on the floor. The wind grates at the walls and what she thinks must be a flock of circling birds caw at the air as it seeps through the cracks in the hastily built walls.

One night, Caroline listens as the caws change pitch and she can hear the sound of the faint screams of childbirth, surely not carried all the way from the village in the valley. Her only contact is the post, which comes scarcely. One morning, she hears a card drop and runs down the winding steps to the flag floor and the door at the bottom of her tower. A single letter sits there and as she turns it over, Caroline sees it is addressed to her sister Danielle, lost for a time perhaps. And then Caroline begins to wonder; wonder where her husband is all the nights he is not with her. The next day Caroline is up and waiting for one of the postman's rare visits, and when he arrives she taps and calls, 'Let me out.'

'What is wrong, Maid?'

'I am locked in.'

'I will get the door open for you. Seems there is a key on the outside inviting anyone in. Easy as anything. There we are.'

With a motion for him to run also, Caroline flees across the fields, over the stile and into her father's arms.

'He told me you were dead, Caroline.'

'Well I'm obviously not and neither do I believe are my sisters.'

'Oh, them.'

'Yes them, like them or not, Father, we must rescue them. Let's go and gather the villagers.'

Caroline drags her father down to the village and they raise the alarm to the Lord of the Manor. The villagers take themselves up the hill to confront Killigrew in his castle. As they reach the doors, he is just coming out of Caroline's tower. Henry tries to flee but the villagers surround him whilst others release the imprisoned brides from the castle. As the crowd close in on Henry, he is cornered and looks set for a beating. He lifts his arms and changes into a large black bird, his beard a beak, his hair a plume.

'Cormorant,' shouts Ince. 'I should've bloody known it.'

'Keep up the chase,' shouts the Lord of the Manor.

'We must punish him,' the daughters agree as they run after the bird. The villagers, heavily armed, take pursuit. On the bank of the River Lynher is a large manikin tree where the cormorants come inland to roost. This is where the sisters are headed, followed by the villagers, their father and the Lord of the Manor, all armed and outraged by Killigrew's deception. The postman hands Caroline his shotgun and she fires along with several others. The King of the Cormorants is three times the size of the other birds and with his wings spread, an easy target as Caroline's shot finds his black heart. The bird lets out an unholy scream and dives, along with his family, into the Dandy Hole. Caroline feels the arms of the postman fit comfortably about her and Farmer Ince wanders back across his boggy fields, hoping there will now be someone handy to cook up a good lunch.

A Ghostly Feast at Bethany

The River Tiddy is a tributary of the Lynher. There are lots of villages and hamlets in the hinterland of its fertile valley including St Germans, Tideford and Bethany. Bethany is near Trerulefoot roundabout between Saltash and Liskeard; it is a hamlet spread along a lane. There is a chapel and a disused school. Walking along the lane there is a smell of freshly cut hedges, the sounds of dogs barking and just out of sight, rushing through the fields, is the train to Plymouth. Farmland surrounds Bethany; fields stretch away into hills. It has a friendly, ordered feel to the hamlet, not at all the place to expect the supernatural to be visiting. However, Dougie Cumming's Granfer knew different.

Bill Cummings was born on a farm in Bethany. Everything appeared as it should about the farm and it was, mostly. Come nightfall, after a hard day's work in the fields, the family shut their doors and settled down for bed. One night, from beneath his covers, young Bill could hear a rattling of cups on the dresser in the kitchen beneath him, a taking down of plates and a clinking of a great many glasses. The kitchen was alive with feasting. People were laughing and singing and shouting. There must have been over 200 people, the noise they were making. Bill's father crept down the stairs to see who was making the tremendous racket. He was feeling rather scared and shaky. But the minute he opened the kitchen door all went quiet. Nobody was there.

The farmer returned to bed thinking it was the night of the summer solstice. When he had settled down to sleep, a sound of clattering crockery and much merrymaking coming from his kitchen woke him up again. Again, the farmer went down the stairs and opened the kitchen door and again, there was silence. No one was to be seen in the kitchen, not one cup was out of place and all was as they had left it. He took a cautious walk around the farmhouse and checked the yard; not one gate was open, every shovel and bucket was in its place and still not a laugh, not a sound.

When the farmer returned to bed, the feasting started again and Farmer Cummings knew there was not a lot he could do but to let whoever it was get on with it. It would be even more challenging than usual to get through the day's work on the farm with no sleep. What had an honest man like himself done to deserve a ghostly intrusion? The farmer, his wife and young Bill were awake until dawn listening to the ghostly banquet. Then all of a sudden, all was quiet and when they went down in the morning it was as if no one had been there at all. Twice a year and always on the

summer solstice, the ghosts came to the farmhouse at Bethany and a ghostly feast occurred. This went on for about ten years and however many times they went down to interrupt, the ghosts would soon start again. One year, Farmer Cummings had had enough. He invited a peller (a wise man who cured ills) to put a spell on his farmhouse so the ghostly feast would never happen again – and sure enough, it didn't.

5

THE LOOE RIVER

'There are more saints in Cornwall than there are in heaven.'

Looe River has two branches; the East and West Looe Rivers. Both rise near Liskeard and flow through secluded and beautiful valleys until they meet the sea. The East Looe River was industrialised during the great commercial activity generated by the mining for copper on Bodmin Moor. A canal ran alongside the East Looe River, once busy in the mining years, as copper ore was transported to Looe to be shipped. The canal has mostly been replaced by the Looe Valley Train. The track runs alongside the river and is the best way to see the fauna in the fields and the birds on the river. Egrets and ducks can be spotted and herons glimpsed from the train. West Looe River is and always has been quieter; when out boating, the river is serene, cloaked by trees. As West Looe River approaches Looe, Kilminorth Woods runs alongside; a peaceful woodland walk from the Millpool in the woods. Beside the river a magical unicorn is painted onto a rock. The East and West Looe Rivers join to create the Looe estuary. The tidal estuary spans back up to Sandplace in the East Looe River and Watergate in the West Looe River.

In spring, the valley fills with a woodland carpet of misty bluebells and swathes of scented wild garlic. All the senses are treated: eyes are caressed by a mass of delicate green lit with a heightening light; ears with the sound of birds and running water; the strong smell of garlic fills the nose and the face is touched by falling blossom and leaf cases. In winter, snowdrops dot the banks and a lone heron flies up and down the valley, silent on the wind.

In the fifth and sixth centuries, saints travelled to Cornwall from Wales and Ireland to tell the Cornish people about Christianity. They built wells over ancient springs at locations already in use for religious practices. Looe River's tales are of Celtic saints and their holy wells. Holy wells are found all over Cornwall and the Looe River has a number of wells not far from its banks. Whether nestling in wooded glens, on the edges of roads or in the middle of a village, the wells have a mystical quality brought about by the sound of spring water on stone. Inside the small granite structures is a quiet stillness and a cool temperature perfect for a moment's contemplation.

On the way up Looe Valley, a peaceful well is blessed by the lovely St Keyne. She began the tradition of newlyweds racing to the well to win the role of master of the marriage. One such bride came from Looe by train; the train was crowded and as she raced her new husband to be first to alight, she fell and broke her neck. Coombe, the little station down the hill from St Keyne Well, is said to be haunted by the poor bride in her wedding gown, trapped on the station platform, searching for the blessing of a virtuous saint.

SAINT KEYNE

Once fifteen brothers and sisters from Wales were sent on their travels to Cornwall. They were very successful in converting the Cornish people to Christianity and were made saints. One sister was exceptionally beautiful; she had leaf-green eyes and deep brown hair. Over time, she became a saint known for performing amazing miracles and possessing a special integrity. The lady was known as St Keyne. She travelled alone and unmolested despite her beauty because she was respected as a saint of virtue.

Having journeyed widely, St Keyne retired to Cornwall. She settled in Looe Valley. The Valley lay shaded by many trees rising from bluebell banks. The East Looe River flowed through flora decked with birds, only widening just as it touched the sea. Like St Keyne, the valley was both beautiful and tranquil. St Keyne loved Looe Valley and she wanted to create a lasting emblem of her stay. She planted four trees around an ancient sacred spring; an oak and an elm side by side, an ash on the bank and a willow to drape the pool. As the trees grew, she entwined the branches to grow as one trunk and shroud the holy well, built above the little spring. She spent most of her time praying and delighting in the beauty of the trees.

Dying, St Keyne was carried to sit by the holy well. The sound of the spring gurgling soothed her and the deep green of the trees reflected back at her through the water. She was grateful for the strength the water gave her and as she lay beside it, St Keyne

blessed the spring. That afternoon she invited a bride and groom, newly married, to sit with her by the well. She held out two goblets and gestured for the couple to each dip one in the spring water. When they had done so and both stood expectant for her example, St Keyne waited, too weak to respond, and the groom thought it polite to gesture for his new wife to drink first. When she had drunk of the clear water of the well, St Keyne told of her last and most eccentric blessing: 'Whichever shall drink first of the Well of St Keyne after their wedding vows, shall be masterful of the marriage and hold the cards to its success.' With this virtue, her dying words, St Keyne was laid to rest, though her trees and her blessing stay with her well to this day.

Saint Cuby

Duloe is a village a mile up a steep, wooded hill from East Looe River. St Cuby's Well is partly hidden by bushes on the edge of Duloe Road. The Victorian novelist and folklorist Mrs Bray described her coach journey down Duloe Hill on the way to Looe, on her visit to the Trelawney family, a road still an experience on the bus today. 'The road is down an abyss, narrow, precipitous, and winds like a cork-screw ... I shall never forget Duloe Hill.' (Trelawney and Trelawne) Opposite the well, on the other side of the road, are fields of apple trees covering the hills. The apples are produced for Cornish Orchards cider and apple juice. Behind St Cuby's Well is Duloe Manor; 300 years ago Duloe Manor was a rectory. The rectors were creative individu-als: Rev. Jeremiah Mills planted an avenue of lime trees still growing outside the house today. Duloe's lime avenue has a mysterious and regal quality about it. A later reverend, Robert Scott, wrote part of the Greek-English-Lexicon (dictionary) at Duloe. He invited his friend Lewis Carroll to stay at the rectory; they were friends from Oxford University. There, Lewis Carroll wrote part of his classic, Alice Through the Looking Glass. *Looe Valley has a magical quality to it and walking through the woods and fields, it feels just the place for a masterpiece of the imagination to have been created.*

Cuby was a Cornish saint and son of Solomon, High King of Cornwall. He learned to read at 7, which might seem a little late, but in those days only those with a religious calling or noble men learned to read. Cuby was both religious and noble. Although he liked making things and playing with his friends, he knew reading was something he wanted to do and he spent hours with a bible balanced on his knee. At 20, Cuby made a pilgrimage to Jerusalem. He loved meeting people along the way, doing new things and converting the particularly stubborn to Christianity. Cuby wasn't a hermit saint; he didn't live and pray alone. He was a sociable saint.

One day, King Solomon died and Cuby was called home to take his throne. Cuby's father had been a chieftain and Christian king of Cornwall but power and rule meant nothing to Cuby. Travel and communication were everything to him, as was his faith. Cuby decided to renounce all claim to the throne and continued on his travels.

He got into lots of trouble on the way – although he meant well, people didn't always appreciate his miraculous powers and his high-handed ways. He lived on Isle of Aran on the west coast of Ireland for a while and caused a calf, and the tree to which it was tied, to be miraculously delivered to himself. The local people didn't like this magic and they drummed him out of the island. He needed a means of escape – he couldn't swim – so he built a quick frame out of bent wood and nailed some planks over. His pursuers jeered. 'If you are really a saint, you will shove her off without skins,' – usually they would stretch skins over a wooden frame to make their currachs. Cuby dared, and the seams were staunch, and he rowed back to Cornwall. St Piran floated to Cornwall on a millstone, St Ia came here in a stone boat but, in spite of himself, St Cuby was the first wooden boat builder.

At one time, he rowed up the tidal river at Looe and found a clearing on the hill nearby. Here he cleared the trees about a fresh spring, the perfect place for a holy well. For a spring to be turned into a holy place, the saint who was founding it must stay on the spot and pray for forty days. Cuby, being a doer and a traveller, found this part of being a religious man very frustrating. His feet itched for the river and the bustle of communication. It was very quiet in the woodland on Kippscoombe Hill and Cuby longed for a challenge or a job to do, so built a chapel out of rough stones found lying about. One of these stones, too large and awkward to fit in any wall, was just right for carving. Sitting daily by the spring, he carved it with his favourite creatures seen on his travels. When Cuby had finished carving he was very pleased with his creation. The little spring flowed into the pretty granite basin, with dolphins engraved about the edge and a griffin on the bottom section. He had made a woodland font. Cuby did not wish the basin to ever be removed from his holy well at Duloe and so he put a curse upon it. Anyone who had the arrogance to take Cuby's basin from its holy site would suffer a terrible comeuppance. Only a man of the greatest strength and conviction would successfully remove it.

For many generations, neighbours of St Cuby's Well respected Cuby's wishes and left the font alone. Then one year, an overconfident farmer tested the curse. He thought the tale about the basin to be folly and knowing himself to be the strongest and bravest Cornish lad for miles about, the farmer hitched up four of his finest oxen to a cart and set off for Duloe and St Cuby's Well. The muscles beneath the gleaming hide on the beasts' bodies rippled with health and strength and the farmer felt himself fill with pride and conviction at the ease of the task ahead. He drummed his fingers on his lips as he thought where best he could place the pretty basin – in his farmyard it would make a good new drinking trough for the cattle, or better still it would make fine new front steps for the farmhouse. As they neared the spot, the farmer looked out across the wooded valley: it really was beautiful and surely wouldn't miss a pretty stone. On reaching the well, the farmer tied strong ropes around the granite basin and hitched them to his team. As he turned to his oxen, his finest ox fell down dead on the ground. The curse had struck and the farmer had lost his greatest beast. Not feeling much more courage left in him, the farmer conceded he must turn back and leave the basin for another.

The farmer could not have been the one Cuby spoke of. Perhaps Cuby envisaged strength of a different kind – a true religious conviction like his own, and the strength to challenge kings and chieftains to take up his beliefs for the people.

SAINT NONA

In West Looe Valley near Pelynt is Hobbs Lane. A hob is a magical creature who farmers knew it was best to have on their good sides, very much like the Cornish piskeys. Off Hobbs Lane can be found Nona's Well. An old oak grows overhead, stone steps lead down to a field and on into the well. Inside is a small round basin covered in moss and full of spring water. Walls are wallpapered with liverwort and hart's-tongue ferns. There are many offerings to the piskey of the well. They are stuffed into crevices and on ledges; a red pouch, fairy dolls, shells, a bottle of syrup, flowers, a heart-shaped button, ribbons and a bracelet. The only sound is of a faint trickle of water. Standing outside the well, feet are surrounded by weeds and reeds, amongst which can be found acorn cups like piskey hats. The field below leads steeply to the wooded valley of West Looe River. A flock of female pheasants fly out of the trees and scatter across the field chirping. Nona's Well is very mysterious, tucked away out of sight in the middle of nowhere.

St Nona, mother of St David, travelled from Wales to visit her sister Wenna. Wenna lived in Morval, a couple of miles inland from Looe. On a beautiful spring day, the two saintly sisters set out to walk the lanes between Morval and Polperro. Bluebells and pink campions filled the floor of the woodland and Nona relished the beauty of nature all about her. Nona and Wenna hitched up their skirts and crossed the West Looe river, then climbed up a steep hill. Midway up the hill was a well. It was 4ft high, covered with a flat stone lintel and an arched roof. Inside, at the far end was a rough, round granite basin, with decorative carvings all around it. The basin was full of fresh sparkling water that entered unseen from the back.

'This is known as Piskey Well,' said Wenna. 'I'll tell you a tale about it. Celtic people called this Piskey Well because they believed it to be guarded by the little people. The piskey was known to have given gifts of health and good fortune to those who respected him and the virtue of his well. Locals revered the Piskey Well. However, he showed great anger to those who dared to desecrate its virtue. The well was protected as it was known the stone in the spring basin could not be moved for fear misfortune would befall those who tried to take it. This is the tale of a farmer who tested their caution.

'One day, the farmer who owned the field with the Piskey Well, decided to use the basin for a better purpose than pleasing the piskey. He thought he might as well use it for a watering trough for his pigs. The farmer took his best oxen to the well and chained them to the basin. He was very surprised when his strongest oxen couldn't move the well. The oxen tired quickly and sweated more than usual. The farmer relented and let them drink from Piskey Well. On their second try the ox pulled the spring basin up the hill but when they were nearing the top, it somehow broke loose from the chains and rolled down the hill, rested a moment and then took a turn to the left and rolled back to the well. Three times the farmer tried to move the basin up the hill to his farm and three times it rolled back down again. The third time, the oxen rolled down the hill after the basin and fell down dead in defeat. The farmer suffered a lifetime of misfortune and became both deaf and lame. No one has ever again thought it wise to move the basin from the Piskey Well.'

When Wenna had finished her tale, the two sisters sat together for some time enjoying the sunshine. Nona was deep in thought. Then she made her decision.

'I wish for this well to be dedicated to me,' said Nona. 'It shall be known as St Nun's Well of Pelynt and I shall guard it as the piskey has done before me.' St Nona was delighted with her well and set about praying for its virtue.

Whilst staying in Cornwall, St Nona founded a monastery at Altarnun on the northern edge of Bodmin Moor. Sadly, with all her good intentions spared, Nona was soon called onwards from her time in Cornwall to Brittany, and somehow the little well became quite forgotten, perhaps because it was situated in the side of a steep hill, accessed only by steps and out of sight from the nearby road. It was left to a farm family owning the land to cut down a huge oak tree that for many years had been growing from the roof of the well, dislodging the stones from the arch with its roots. As they were clearing away the tree and cutting it for wood, they found, to their great delight, the well. The farmer and his family rebuilt St Nun's Well's stony structure and cleaned out the mouldy cell inside. Perhaps it was St Nona who encouraged them in this task of restoration. The oak regrew and shades the well to this day and green moss clothes the walls inside. The basin is still full of sparkling water that enters the well unseen, and as for the piskey … who knows?

THE LISKEARD POEM

'The South wind always brings fine weather
The North wind wet and cold together
The West wind always brings the rain
The East wind blows it back again.'

THE PIPEWELL STORIES

Just above the Looe River at the beginning of the Looe Valley train line is Liskeard. Liskeard is a town of strong grey architecture. Every shop has a proud building looming above it. There are many gift shops, useful shops and eateries. Walking down the streets, the clock tower chimes the hour. Liskeard was a stannary town with metals being brought in from mines on Bodmin Moor; South Caradon, East and West Caradon, Marke Valley and Gonamena to be weighed and sold. The town still has a feeling of lost importance as if, amongst all the grand buildings, a long-gone lifestyle might once again be found. Until December 2017, Liskeard was also a market town; the large cattle market served the farms for miles around from the moors to the sea. Cows could be heard across town as the cattle market car park filled with buyers and sellers, large vehicles and crowds on foot. As it loses its status as the centre for the farming community, much talk takes place over what the market place will become – a shopping centre, a car park or a community centre. In Well Lane is a medieval spring housed by the Pipe Well. The Pipewell tale tells a promise of how a happy marriage and a healing spring are all a town would need. With the market gone, perhaps the Pipewell will once again be the focal point of Liskeard Town.

It's late afternoon and Mr Kekewich is admiring the four iron pipes he has bought and had specially fitted to the four plentiful springs of St Martin's Well in Liskeard. He rubs his chin as he turns to the gathered crowd.

'My uncle, John Trehawke, would turn in his grave if he could see his carefully hoarded fortune splashed out for all to admire. Well I tell you, it's my inheritance and I shall spend it as it suits me. The well deserves a bit of industry and these pipes are grand as I can get. I believe it deserves a new name too. All you good people of Liskeard, I rename your well Pipewell.'

A cheer goes out to Kekewich, the crowd enjoying his bravado. A voice lingers after the applause.

'You may mark my words, Mr Kekewich. Adding to all the grandness of they buildings ain't going to bring back what this well is known for; the magic healing powers it can give and its lucky stone.'

Kekewich looks at the lady a moment; she is old as the stone, his aunt perhaps or his aunt's aunt's aunt.

'Look all you like, maid,' he says firmly, 'but I tell you what I see: four smart iron pipes and four gushing springs, a nice pool and no stone.'

The elderly lady looks back at Kekewich with her sharp brown eyes. 'I can tell you all a tale, one you should rightly know,' she licks her lips excited.

'St Martin's Well has been used for its healing qualities since the Celts first came down off the moors and settled here. When I was a maid betrothed to be married, I came here with my husband-to-be. We stood on the lucky stone together and drank water from the chief spring. My mother told me that if I touched the stone with my bare feet then we would have a good future and by drinking together we would be happy and successful in our married life. Times were every betrothed maid in Liskeard came here to make her wish. We believed every word of it. We had been blessed by the well nymph and the truth be told we were happy, very happy and blessed. It was said the lucky stone gave magical powers to anyone who touched it. I don't know about that. I don't think of myself as particularly magical; we simply valued the powers of the spring. Imagine, a healing spring and a promise of a happy marriage. What more could a town need? Every generation has respected St Martin's Well and they looked after it proper until recent times. You only have to look at the building you see above it as proof enough to that. Then this here new council claimed the stone had 'lost its virtue' and they goes and covers it up putting an end to all the good fortune and free blessing us folks of Liskeard got from the waters whenever we so pleased. Now you are no better, Kekewich, you have sheathed the water. Iron won't stay like that mind and before long we won't even be safe to drink it. Real shame that is, real shame.'

Kekewich took a deep breath from his stomach. 'Don't you worry about the quality of the water, lady. It's discharging three gallons a minute and they say it has never yet run dry.' The elderley lady turned away from the revelling crowd. Her piece was said. She would never again visit the well.

Now it may be that you have listened carefully to the value in the elderly lady's speech and you believe luck to be more valuable than iron? It may be that you are living in Liskeard town and are brave enough to take away the pipes and restore the holy well? Perhaps you would like to have the lucky stone retrieved from the concrete for surely a promise of a prosperity and happy families is priceless to your community?

But above all, wouldn't it be great to attract visitors from all over the world to Liskeard to drink the crystal clear water … and charge £6 a glass to do so!

TALES FROM
BODMIN MOOR

6

CARADON HILL

'Jack the lantern,
Joan the Wad
Light me home
The weather's bad.'

Bodmin Moor has many tales attached to its wild and mysterious landscape; tales of giants, angels, druids and a piskey. From Liskeard the land rises steeply to the moor at Cornwall's highest village, Minions. The path towards the Cheesewring from Minions up Stowes Hill is a stone track edged by mossy, waterlogged grass. On one side of the track are the grassed-over remains of mine buildings. A serpent's back of grassy cairns leads up to the Rillaton Barrow. On the other side of Minions, on Craddock Moor are three stone circles known locally as the Hurlers. Black stunted hawthorns stand against blue grey cloud. Wind circles, it buffets the ears and rakes the earth. The sky is vast as is the horizon. The eye travels across mine chimneys, fields, woods, towns, to the looming shapes of Dartmoor. When it comes into sight, the Cheesewring stands, a huge pile of dark granite, majestic against the winter sky. One side of Stowe's Hill is covered in granite clitter cascading down to the Withybrook Marsh; the other is eaten by quarrying.

The Legend of the Cheesewring

It was at the time when Christianity had not been long in Cornwall. Saints built stone houses over the wells and declared them sacred. They scattered the fields with stone crosses. You would have perhaps expected the people to be wary of the incoming faith. Instead, they began to bring the saints gifts of fish on Fridays. This gesture of acceptance angered the giants who had dominated the lands for centuries. Giants were not fond of stone

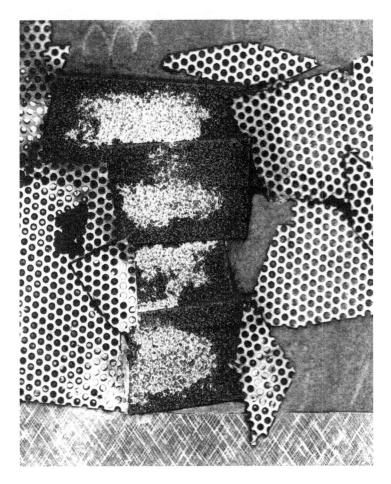

crosses or the occupation of the wells by men, and they were especially irritated by the taxes charged by the saints for the use of the land. Giants were used to stomping over whatever ground they pleased, and hurling whichever rocks they pleased, carved with a cross or no.

At that time the strongest and most fearless giant was named Uther and the giants nominated him for the task of ridding Cornwall of saints. They called a council up on the high moor and invited the saints to send a representative. It was a damp day and dark clouds gathered. Soon the marshes would spread and the mist fall. Not the day for a small and weak-chested saint to venture amongst the gigantic muddy boots filling the moor. When Uther spied tiny St Tue weaving his way bravely toward him, he felt a surge of generosity. He lifted St Tue on to the palm of his hand so they could enter into council.

Now St Tue had climbed many steep hills on the way to the Giant Council and all the way he had been considering a plan. He breathed deep in his tummy and forced himself to look up at the hideous giant.

'I come with a challenge for you, mighty Uther,' he said. 'To a stone throwing contest.'

Uther smiled down at the tiny saint who dared challenge the greatest giant. 'I will hear your challenge,' Uther replied, feeling amicable.

'I challenge you to a duel of strength,' St Tue replied.

There was a rumble of muffled thunder ribbing across the moor as the giants passed the message of the tiny saint's folly.

'And what of this challenge, St Tue?' Uther asked.

'If you triumph you will rid the land of saints in one fair contest. If I win, you and all the other giants present across Stowe's Hill and Craddock Moor shall convert to Christianity. For there is one, the Almighty, who is stronger than you all.'

Now, all the giants of the land were gathered at Uther's council and not one believed this to be a challenge to be lost. For each giant considered himself to be incredibly strong and each knew Uther was the strongest of them all and therefore very, very strong indeed. St Tue on the other hand, was visibly frail even for a saint and they had never seen any saint looking all mighty. The giants all loved throwing rocks. They began to feel quite cheerful at the prospect of a hurling celebration.

The terms of the contest were agreed. There were to be twelve quoit-sized rocks, six for each side. These were to be hurled across Craddock Moor and onto Stowe's Hill. The giants delighted in finding the biggest rocks. St Tue said nothing in protest. When the rocks were gathered ready, Uther picked up the first rock and hurled it as far as he could up onto the hill. St Tue looked down and put his hands against either side of the next rock. It felt cold and damp. St Tue was sure his skin would graze as he tried to lift the grey and unforgiving weight. Drawing upon his faith, St Tue was amazed for the stone felt light as a feather. He held it, balanced and aimed to place the stone upon Uther's. St Tue threw his stone. There were shouts from the giants and they turned to encourage the giant Uther to get on with his next piece. Uther threw it easily and a third stone balanced on the pile. St Tue took his stone more confidently and they continued until the two largest stones remained.

Uther had only to throw the thirteenth and spare stone and he would rid Cornwall of saints forever. It was a very heavy stone, and Uther knew his strength was spent. He took the boulder and threw it anyway, and it hit the side of the hill and rolled down. The giants roared in anguish. Then it was St Tue's final throw; Uther had his part completed. St Tue balanced his stone, and the giants roared louder, trying to unsettle the saint. St Tue gathered his small strength and as he lifted the stone an angel came and held it for him, balancing it ever so carefully on top of the pile with his beautiful golden wings. The giants saw a strong ray of sunlight break through the clouds and light the moor all about the strangely balancing pile of stones; a rock pile crowned with St Tue's last stone. Christianity was here to stay in Cornwall.

Uther was so amazed that he asked St Tue to baptise him there and then. The other giants took a little longer to accept the results of the contest. Some were baptised, but many others chose to leave Cornwall to the saints.

THE ANGEL AND THE COCKEREL

Each day Mrs Harris's garden filled with orange – the orange brown of autumn leaves. It was summer at Minions and if you came up onto the moors and looked closer, you would have seen the orange brown feathers of Crispin Cockerel and his hens. The garden was large enough for the hens to have a different space to scratch in at different times of day.

Every morning, as dawn broke across Bodmin Moor, it was Crispin's special job to tell everyone in the parishes that day had come. Now on this particular morning, Crispin was awake early. It was still a while before he needed to do his job and tell Minions about the day but he felt his chest swelling with excitement and he really wanted to shout about the lovely morning that was coming. Crispin had always been a naughty and loud cockerel and he was in a very talkative mood, but even he knew that Mrs Harris would have him for dinner if he crowed before the sun. Then Crispin had an idea, and he half leapt, half flew over the fence and took himself on an adventure across the moors.

Feeling so happy with his hens and his moor, he ran as fast as he could, shouting to the nesting birds and the stunted trees, until he was almost at the top of Stowe's Hill and just beneath the Cheesewring.

As dawn broke golden and clear across the grateful moor, Crispin puffed with warmth and pride and joy at the sight of the sun. He shouted and shouted as loud as he could, to let the villagers know the day had come, but his voice couldn't reach them. Crispin felt his tail feathers droop; he had failed in his very own task. He looked up at the Cheesewring with its solemn stones and he couldn't believe his beak. An angel with wings made from the gold of the morning light was lifting up the top rock of the Cheesewring. As Crispin Cockerel watched in amazement from the grass below, the angel turned the top rock three times and then stayed a moment longer to talk to Crispin.

'Crispin,' said the angel. 'Your job is of great importance and I know you have good intentions. If ever again you have wandered across the moors and it's time for your morning job, come to the Cheesewring to crow. I will turn the stone so the villagers of the surrounding parishes will see it turning and they will know the sign that dawn has come.'

To this day, sometimes, just sometimes, as the day breaks over the moor and the cockerel crows to welcome the day, the stone at the top of the Cheesewring turns around once, twice, three times, and the grey moor is touched with the gold of a glimpse of an angel's wings.

THE RILLATON CUP

A druid sat on his daily seat offering a drink to all who passed by. He held a beautiful gold cup that would mysteriously refill after every drink. One day, three huntsmen rode across the marshes. The druid offered them a drink and each rider drank a long draft, as it had been a hard ride across the moors. The third huntsman drank and drank until he felt quite sick and still the druid's cup was full of a fine golden liquid. The huntsman became angry the cup wouldn't empty. He spat out the wine, threw some at the startled druid and galloped off with the cup in his hand. The huntsman didn't get far; his horse stumbled as it ran over and down the stony hill. The huntsman tumbled off and cracked his head, dented his skull, broke his bones. The cup landed soft in a grassy hollow – no cracks or breaks or dents to mar its gold.

Many years later, the huntsman was found buried in a barrow, the cup lay by his side along with a bronze sword. For a while it was used as a shaving mug by a king, but today the druid's cup is kept very safe in a museum. It's now known as the Rillaton Cup, but without the druid, it remains empty to this day.

THE OLD STORM WOMAN

Across the moor from Minions in the parish of St Neot, is Dozmary Pool. Dozmary Pool is a friendly place, high on the moor yet not desolate, the kind of place to have a helpful serene being; the Lady of the Lake of King Arthur's tales. The ground around the pool is peat bog and marshland with reeds and ducks and golden gorse. It is not a lake to easily walk around; Dozmary is wild wetland. Light reflects off the water and the strong moorland wind makes many waves. On a stormy night the voice of Tregeagle carries on the wind. It is the spirit of the wind I am going to tell, in the tale of the Old Storm Woman, who creates the winds of the world beneath Dozmary Pool.

High on Bodmin Moor lays Dozmary Pool, a drop of the sea, a place said to be the source of wind. Beneath its surface the Old Storm Woman, an incredibly old woman – older than your great, great granny – concocts a wind especially for each new day.

She stirs it deep beneath the waters with a huge weather stirrer.

Small strokes to begin, increasing until she has conjured a whirlpool in the centre of the pool. When it is ready and moving well, the old woman screws up her terribly old face, until every wrinkle is deep as a ditch and blows.

The water fights, swirling and bursting with the force of the wind.

With a rush the new wind rises up from the depths of the lake, through the vortex of the whirlpool to fill the moorland skies.

PISKEY LED

On Bodmin Moor around Jamaica Inn, farmland and moorland overlap, as do the paths of farmer and piskey. There is a saying on Bodmin Moor to be 'Piskey Led'. Piskey Led is when the piskeys lead travellers or farmers astray on the moors. Piskey Led people are 'Mazed' (confused and disorientated, lost). Even in a place known well, the unfortunate person won't be able to find their way. Luckily, there is a cure for being mazed: simply turn your pockets inside out, or socks, jacket, hat. Even better, never venture out on the moor without first turning your socks and your pockets inside out, then you will be one step ahead of the piskeys.

John and William Bray were out on the moor, counting their grazing cattle. The cattle were roaming free up on the common land for the summer season. It had been one of those years when the rain kept coming, the drains overflowed and the grass went squelch underfoot. Along the way the two men laughed together as they climbed hedges and jumped squirting springs and flooded lanes. Up on the moor this state of saturation was accentuated even more than in the villages. In late summer, the bogs were usually dried and stuffed full with peering reeds. In contrast, this year the bogs were filling up from the underground spilling springs, gullies and miners' caverns. Beneath the earth and rock sat a hidden sea. Anyone who had business out in the marshes like John and William had best tread with care on the stepping stones and firmer patches of ground.

John could see a good amount of his black-bellied cows and as he came over a hill, a herd of moorland horses galloped by. He threw his stick after them, urging them away from the water, but unbeknownst to William, the horses belonged to piskeys. Tiny stirrups could just be seen plaited into the horses' manes. The stirrups twinkled like stars in the flapping manes as the horses ran off down the hill. Standing on a granite rock nearby was a ring of piskeys who had been about to mount their horses. The piskeys stamped their boots in frustration and looked angrily about for the cause of their horses' sudden flight.

Whatever you do, you don't want to make a piskey angry, for they play tricks on those who displease them.

John had already begun to walk home and William went to follow him, taking a safe path they knew so well; a safe path they took daily through the treacherous bog.

All of a sudden, John sunk to his waist in the black watery slime. He thought he would find a rock ledge to use as an anchor, as he usually did if he missed his footing in such a manner. Strangely there was nothing but more loose mud beneath him: mud, thick as treacle, slimy as syrup, a treacherous pond pudding. John couldn't move his legs; they were stuck fast. He tried to scissor-kick free, but scissors don't cut mud. John had begun to feel truly mazed by his sudden predicament, confused and scared: he thought he would be swallowed by the bog and found in a thousand years' time, perfectly preserved, his farmer's hat still on his head, his farmer's boots still tightly laced.

Quick as a fairy's flash, William remembered the stout wooden stick he always carried with him on such journeys. William held it out across the bog and John began to wriggle his torso toward it. Scraping with his fingers across the slimy, weedy surface was most unpleasant. All the while he felt as if the piskey huntsmen were hooting with laughter at their revenge on poor, muddy, mazed John.

Well, after much strain John managed to grab the stick. William heaved and William pulled – William's arms were tough as tin, hard as the oak trees he sawed for firewood each winter. Both of John's arms lay stretched across the surface

– arms brawny from bale throwing, sturdy from stone walling, and he clamped them to the heavy stick. William pulled and John held fast and … SQUELCH …

John was winched out of the muddy bog. He slid along the surface, holding onto the stick for dear life until he felt firmer land beneath his belly.

'I was piskey led, I tell 'ee, that's what it was.'

'Piskey nothing, you'm mazed by they, not led by they. Just a bit of mud, John.'

'Stealing our horses, they were. Have to keep a closer look on the cattle we've got up here from now on.'

'That as may be John, that as may be.'

'Luck as have it, I put my socks on inside out this morning …'

As William and John walked home across the moor, the latter cold and muddy but glad to be alive, they were watched by tens of tiny folk. Tiny folk hiding in the gorse bushes, behind the rocks, beneath the moor ferns. Tiny folk who may be watching you when you go for a walk on the moor …

So, if you feel yourself getting lost or mazed while out walking, just turn your pockets inside out and you'll be safe.

Figgy Hobbin

South Caradon Mine is an area on the south-western side of Caradon Hill. Caradon Mining District was made a World Heritage Site in 2006. The Caradon Hill Area Heritage Project worked from 2008 to 2016 restoring the crumbling mine buildings. Rule's Shaft Engine House of South Caradon Mine has a stunning window visible across the moor, the stonework beautifully repointed. Next to the engine house is the blocked off Tramway Tunnel and a bank of huge slag heaps to the side. Copper mining was at its height from 1840 to the 1890s; in 1836 a lot of copper was found at South Caradon. The mine was owned by Captain James Clemo and the Kittow family. Today the moor is ferns with some stunted trees and many sheep. Looking across the fields, the sea is on the horizon. Much of the Caradon mining area is rocks and slag heaps; these are known locally as 'The Crystal Mines' where children search in the rubble for fool's gold, quartz and ore in the rocks.

Sam Hambly was a young miner who lived with ten members of his family in a tiny cottage in St Cleer. The interior was cold and damp and crowded and Sam had to fight for anything and everything. Because of his overcrowded home, Sam much preferred being out and about on the moor. Early each morning, he would thank his mother for the pasty she gave him and walk the few miles up to Caradon Hill, where he worked up South Caradon, mining copper. Sam knew his pasty would be lean, the pastry stretched thin and the potatoes rubbery. Shoving it deep into his pockets, he set out for the mine. If his luck was in, he would be eating something much tastier for his crib (snack). Sam scrambled over the stony path, up past Trethevy Quoit, across the fields to the Crows Nest and up the track to the mines. As the moor opened up before him, Sam saw her, Rosemary Harvey, the loveliest bal maiden. Rosemary Harvey worked as a cobber at the copper mine. In one hand she carried a short hammer she used to break the ore into little pieces; in the other hand she carried a carefully wrapped parcel. Sam tried to keep his gaze on Rosemary but he couldn't help peeking at

the parcel. Nineteen-year-old Rosemary was a brilliant cook and made the best figgie hobbin Sam had ever tasted. She smiled shyly at Sam and he gave her his broadest grin in return. Walking side by side, they crossed the rest of the moor together. Sam worked a long way underground and Rosemary worked on the surface. As they parted, Rosemary gave Sam the parcel of her freshly made figgie hobbin and he felt like the luckiest miner alive.

It took a while to make his way down the slippery ladders deep into the mine. The load had been scant recently and Sam decided to make his way down a different tunnel to his team. The rock was hard and unforgiving but Sam wasn't going to give in. He had made the decision to work here and he would keep tapping with his pick; perhaps he would find the richest load in Cornwall. Working for hours, he began to feel more and more foolish. After a time, the very rock began to echo his efforts. Knock, knock, knock went Sam Hambly's pick and knock, knock, knock echoed the mine. He became convinced someone was working directly opposite him on the other side of the rock. Indeed, they were; tiny mine beings called knockers were mimicking the sound of Sam's pick.

'Be gone with you, knockers. Today I want to work alone,' Sam shouted. His voice echoed back at him mingled with the knockers' laughter.

With the work of all the picks in Cornwall, Sam began to doubt anything much would come from this rock. Then all at once he had it, right in front of him; the richest load he had ever come across. He went to work to extract as much ore as he could. He would be rich in no time, rich enough to ask for Rosemary's hand in marriage. At last Sam sunk down in exhaustion; it was time for crib. He unraveled the hobbin. It looked delicious. He brought it close to his face and smelt it, yummy. Just as he was about to take a bite of his hobbin, Sam heard voices all about him.

'Sam Hambly, Sam Hambly
Give us some of your 'obbin
or bad luck to thee tomorrow.'

But Sam didn't want to share even one crumb of his hobbin. With every bite he was hungrier than the last and he woofed it down until there was not even one crumb left. Licking his fingers, Sam went back to work. He felt excited and positive; not only had he found copper all by himself, he was to be married and his Rosemary would be proud of him as he was of her. Just as he was tidying his tools ready for him to return to the load in the morning, he heard the knockers again.

'Sam Hambly, Sam Hambly,

We'll send you bad luck tomorrow

Eat all your 'obbin and you'll be sobbin'.'

And it was then Sam began to regret not leaving a crumb of his crib for the knockers. It was tradition down the mine and he had left the knockers at least a crumb most days. But when it had really mattered and the knockers had needed thanking for finding him such a rich load, he had greedily left them nothing and he would pay for it, of that he was sure. Sam turned his back on his day's work and wearily climbed the ladders and set off across the dark moors for home.

Next day, Sam returned to the mine with a sense of foreboding. He couldn't bring himself to even raise his eyes in greeting to Rosemary as she stood waiting for him at the gateway to the moor. They walked together in silence. Every moment Sam wished he could tell her about the incredible load he had found the previous day. He kept thinking to tell her and then something stopped him. Perhaps she would think him foolish with his superstitions and tales of the knockers. He didn't want to get her hopes up. The knockers had told him he would have bad luck and he thought they were probably right.

Reaching the tunnel where he had left his tools, Sam's heart sank. Where just the night before had been a rich load of ore lay a huge pile of boulders blocking his way. A crumb of Figgie Hobbin, just one crumb left for the knockers of the mine and they would have continued to help him to become a rich man. Having eaten every last bit of Rosemary's Figgie Hobbin, Sam was left with nothing. He couldn't continue working as a miner knowing what he had found and lost. He shoved his hands deep into his pockets, felt yesterday's pasty with his fingertips. He could have given the knockers his pasty. Should've given them his pasty. He pulled the pasty out of his pocket and left it on the nearest boulder. Perhaps he would have to become a farm labourer and leave the mine to the knockers. Sam hurried back up the slippery ladder and home.

BODMIN MOOR: THE MOOR'S EDGE

'Look out, look out,
The beast is about.'

Early settlers cleared forest and cultivated the moor. A change in climate meant they moved down into the valleys and built villages and enclosures. The Celts began a practice of grazing their cattle on the high moor in summer and bringing them down to pasture in the lowlands in colder winter months, a practice used by farmers ever since. Nowadays, there are many farms, villages and towns existing on the edge of the moors. It used to be the cows would wander the villages and eat the tastiest plants belonging to unsuspecting gardeners; now cattle grids are used to discourage them. The tales of the moor's edge are of helpful and busy piskeys, a pair of hunting kings, and of the many shapes and sizes of the elusive Beast of Bodmin.

THE PISKEYS AND THE HOUSEWORK

Long ago, a young girl named Tegan (who was named after a Cornish queen) was invited to stay with her Great Aunt Chesten, who lived in a cottage near Liskeard on the edge of Bodmin Moor. In those days it wasn't often a child was invited away and Tegan's mother made a big fuss in preparing her.

'You must be polite and helpful at all times, Tegan. Helpful, yes that is what I want you to be. An elderly lady like Aunt Chesten shouldn't be doing all her housework alone.'

'Yes, Mother,' Tegan assured her.

Tegan's mother turned to her husband, who was busy shaving wood off a swollen door. 'Aunt Chesten has a large pot of gold at her house. If the old woman takes a liking to our Tegan, we will get a good share of gold when she dies.'

Her husband didn't comment, preferring to stare intently along the wood. When at last Tegan was ready with a sack of clothes and some cake for her great aunt, she set out in the direction of Liskeard.

The moors about were windy and wild but to Tegan's surprise, Great Aunt Chesten's home was perfectly ordered and smelt of fresh flowers. A good supper was ready in a big black pot on the stove, welcome as Tegan felt very hungry after her journey. Before she went to bed, Tegan remembered her mother's request and said, 'Could you please wake me early, Great Aunt Chesten, I would like to help with the chores.'

'Goodnight, Tegan,' was all her great aunt replied.

Tegan was tired out and slept well in the little bed in the damp spare room. When she woke up and ran down to help, breakfast was all laid and her great aunt was sitting by a crackling fire. Tegan spent the day exploring the fields and moorland surrounding the cottage. She again enjoyed a good supper and asked to be woken especially early to be of use with lighting the fire and any heavy lifting. Great Aunt Chesten just smiled and said goodnight and the little girl left the elderly lady rocking in her chair.

She woke to the sound of Great Aunt Chesten calling her to breakfast. Downstairs, Tegan looked about her and again all the chores had been done.

'You seem very worried about the chores, Tegan,' teased her great aunt. 'I am very pleased they are all done myself.'

It was then Tegan decided to admit her mother's request.

'Mother says I must be very helpful,' she said, rather crestfallen at the silliness of her position.

'The piskeys did all the housework long before you were up.'

'Piskeys? What are piskeys?'

'Piskeys are fairies of course, our own Cornish fairies. You cannot have the piskey sight if you have got to your age and don't even know about them. Piskeys are all over South East Cornwall, my lovely. It's a shame you'll never see them.'

'Oh, I must,' said Tegan excited. 'Please, Great Aunt Chesten, how might I?'

'Well now, piskey sight can sometimes be gained by looking through a four-leaf clover. They won't like it mind. Piskeys enjoy being helpful but prefer you let them get on with things and don't even like a thanking.'

Tegan ate the rest of her boiled eggs in silence and then slipped outside to search the fields for a four-leaf clover. She couldn't find one anywhere, even though the fields were rich with clover. The plants all had three leaves and the cows happily ate it in bunches. She hardly slept that night and woke very early. Standing by the kitchen door, Tegan peered through the keyhole. She could hear a lot of bustling about and the pots and pans clanging together. She even thought she could hear the wood basket being dragged across the floor.

But Tegan couldn't see any piskeys. In fact, the only thing she could see strolling about the kitchen was Great Aunt Chesten's big, fluffy cat. As she leaned on the door to see closer, Tegan came crashing into the kitchen. The piskeys stopped in annoyance and ran away, leaving half the work undone. Great Aunt Chesten came downstairs very grumpy. The old woman set about finishing the chores herself, leaving Tegan to stand around feeling awkward.

Escaping, Tegan set out over the fields in search once more of a four-leaf clover. The fields were full of buttercups. Tegan thought she might pick a lovely bunch so her aunt might forgive her for disturbing the piskeys. As she was arranging and rearranging the blooms and delighting at the flowers, Tegan heard the cat meowing at her from a little way across the field. Expecting her to have caught a shrew, Tegan walked over to inspect the cat's find. Beneath its fluffy paw was a perfect four-leaf clover. Aunt Chesten's cat had found Tegan the key to piskey sight.

On the fourth morning of her stay, Tegan clutched the clover leaf and waited with impatience. At last, she thought she heard the sounds of piskeys doing the housework. Tegan hurried downstairs with her treasure and held it up before the keyhole.

Tegan looked through the four-leaf clover and it was exactly as Great Aunt Chesten had said: piskeys were everywhere. Tiny men with pea green suits and bright dark eyes, brushed the floor and mopped it. They carried in the heavy log basket between twenty of them or more and easily started a very good fire. Piskeys washed the dishes and scrubbed the pots. Tegan watched as they leapt on one another's shoulders creating a wobbly piskey tower and began to pass up the big black pots to hang from their hooks high on the walls. Just as the last pan was halfway up, the bottom piskey fell to his knees and they all came tumbling down. The piskeys looked so comical, grimacing and checking their elbows for grazes that Tegan laughed very loudly. Seeing them looking to one another in alarm, she tried to hold her hands over her mouth to stifle the giggles.

'The girl has piskey sight and she is watching piskey work. We will not stay here another day,' they said in chorus.

'There are plenty of other elderly people needing our help without nosy girls.'

And with that command, all the piskeys ran out of the house never to return. Great Aunt Chesten was grumpy again and sent Tegan home. When she died shortly after, the elderly lady left her gold to strangers and Tegan learned never, never to interfere with another lady's housework.

KING ALFRED AND KING DUNGARTH

St Neot is a moorland village just a few miles from Dozmary Pool. A quiet village with a church, a school and a social club, it is renowned in South East Cornwall for its vibrant sense of community and everyone who moves to St Neot talks about their village with pride. There is an active historical society in St Neot; a group of players perform a pantomime every winter and concerts and community plays take place regularly. The village has a community garden and park. Over a bridge and along a track leading out of the village is the way to St Neot's Holy Well. The path runs alongside the Loveny River and opens out into a boggy field of reeds. To access the holy well, wellington boots are necessary. Restored in 1862, the well is enclosed by a small stone building with a stone cross on top. It has a wooden doorway and latch. The field surrounding the well is calm and sheltered from the wind by a steep bank and trees. Sunlight glitters through branches overhanging the river. Birdsong fills the field and a crow flies across into trees. Once a king came to visit.

King Alfred loved to hunt and often came down to Cornwall to take advantage of the swathes of moorland surrounding Liskeard. He stayed in Liskeard with his friend Dungarth, King of Cornwall, and visited his oldest brother Neot, who lived nearby. A man of very short stature, Neot was a hermit who spent his days praying by a sacred, healing spring. He was himself greatly respected for his healing powers.

One day, the kings were up on the moors hunting red deer. They had been riding since morning and it was well into the afternoon when King Alfred began feeling unwell.

'I am sorry, dear Dungarth, I fear I cannot go on.'

'You are of a sickly disposition, my friend, but surely you can ride to the edge of the moors? Once there, we will fetch your brother, Neot.'

'You are right. I will follow you but not at the reckless gallop I usually enjoy.'

'Don't you fear, Alfred.'

Dungarth kicked his horse into a canter and they took off across the heather, over Bron Wennihi, 'Hill of Swallows', Cornwall's highest tor, then into a smooth gallop as they took on the open moorland between Bron Wennihi and Dozmary Pool. Alfred felt dizzy and sick as he clung to his horse. This was a gentle gallop after all and they were sticking to the sheep paths, rather than leaping lumps of granite and gorse. King Alfred was a weak man and often unwell, but he knew his brother would be able to heal him.

When they got to the well on the edge of the moors, Alfred slid from his horse, tired and ill. Neot the tiny saint asked Dungarth to help his fading friend into a kneeling position and they all three prayed together. A little red deer walked shyly across the clearing and nuzzled Neot as he knelt. He motioned for the kings to lay aside their hunting souls, for Neot was a friend to all the birds and animals of the Cornish countryside. The little red deer wandered down to the river to drink.

'My stomach still hurts so badly, brother,' said Alfred, watching the deer.

'How many burnt cakes you been eating, Alfred?' asked Dungarth.

'Not another word about burning a poor woman's cakes!'

'You ate them all as they were, though. Didn't you?'

'That I did.'

'Was most likely the start of all your sickness.'

'Enough of your banter, we must bathe Alfred, and trust in faith,' said Neot.

King Alfred was bathed in the healing waters of the well and St Neot spoke gently to him, encouraging him; he would soon be revived. So strong was Alfred's faith in his brother's healing powers, he was indeed revived and felt stronger than he had for months. From that day onwards, King Alfred's visits to Liskeard were for both hunting and healing. Alfred had a special granite cross carved with Celtic knotwork in gratitude to Neot for his kindness. The cross stands in St Neot's churchyard to this day.

Sadly, the exuberant hunting trips of King Dungarth and King Alfred ended in tragedy. In 875 King Dungarth drowned in the River Fowey at Golitha Falls while out hunting. In the parish of St Cleer, by the side of the road near Golitha, are two fragments of granite pillars or half stones. One is 8ft high, carved over with knotwork. 'The Other Half Stone' is a plinth with knotwork of Celtic patterns covering three sides with an inscription in Latin on the fourth which translates as 'Doniert asks you to pray for his soul.'

The pillar is placed on the edge of a field next to 'Two Cross Downs' where an ancient crossroads once took an important place on the moors. The main tracks through Cornwall joining Plymouth, Bodmin and Launceston crossed here and the memorial would have been visited by crowds of those travelling through Cornwall to pay their respects and pray for the soul of Cornwall's great King Dungarth. It is a very ornate and carefully engraved stone and there is a chance King Alfred had it specially made for his friend, who was the last king of Cornwall.

THE PHANTOM BEAST

In the roads and farms around the edges of the moor and in many places on the high moor itself, there have been sightings of the Bodmin Beast. An animal the size of a puma has been seen on a number of separate occasions and tracks have been left but no one has found the animal's home or her cubs. Once a skull was found in the River Fowey at Golitha but after much examination it turned out to be imported. The Bodmin Beast takes on a mystical and mythical quality. No one knows for sure whether or not a giant cat roams Bodmin Moor. Great ghostly dogs have also been spotted on the moors. Hounds chase Tregeagle across Bodmin Moor and Dando and his Dogs run howling all over Cornwall. The Darley Dog, the ghost of Vincent Darley, appears in the road between Darley Ford and North Hill. A great black dog with shining eyes, the Darley Dog appears in the road, terrifying all who encounter him, then strides past and off into the night. The Bodmin Beast definitely lives on as a recurring phantom of folk memory and the more it is sighted, the more people believe in its existence.

Rob Mitchell was walking home along the road from Callington. Trees grew from the hedges and spread black threads against the sky. Dark clouds rolled across the moors and settled behind the trees. Rob thought perhaps he saw a flicker of a bat, melting as a snowflake into the dark. Movement within the shades of darkness could have been a fox; too quick a shadow to focus into form. He kept his eyes strained nervously in front of him. Then the very

clear shadow of a giant cat, lithe and alert, quivering but silent, stood before Rob in the middle of the road.

The predator paused and glared at Rob with gorse yellow eyes before crouching to leap the hedge and was away across the fields. Rob got out his torch, thinking he might find a claw print beneath the hedge or a snag of fur, but the hedge was high with vegetation. Climbing up the bank, he imagined a fair few stems of bracken were bent across the field. A cold wind pushed into Rob's back and he swung round with his torch shining down on the empty road.

Next morning, Rob went for a walk around about to see who he could tell. *It's a good story this one,* he thought with excitement. He had met the Beast, a phantom beast, even better. However, everyone Rob met that day to tell his story of the phantom beast had also seen the Beast in their lane, behind their car or up the moor and one even had a cast of its claw print left in his garden.

THE PISKEY WHO LOST HIS LAUGH

In the next story many tales link together as a piskey makes a journey. 'The Piskey Who Lost his Laugh' is a tale travelling all through Caradon. Caradon is the old name for South East Cornwall.

One night a ring of piskeys danced on tufted grass at the site of King Arthur's court at Gelliwig. They fell in a dizzy heap laughing together. A piskey called Pasco was silent; he kept trying to laugh with the others but found he couldn't. It is very unusual for a piskey to be silent and the others soon noticed.

'What is a piskey without a laugh?' they jeered. The piskeys relinked their arms in a new ring, leaving poor Pasco out.

Pasco was very sad. All he wanted now was to find his laugh. He tumbled down hill into a pile of soft earth. In the darkness he heard a scolding voice.

'Do you know how long it took to build this mound?'

'Sorry, I fell in. Who are you?'

'I am a mole.'

'You sound very posh for a mole.'

'I am the fallen Lady Want.'

'Fallen from what?'

'From King Arthur's court of course, not that it matters. I've never met a solemn or lonely piskey. What happened to you?'

'Oh Mole, I'm so sad. I've lost my laugh.'

'Piskey, I know just who can help you. Travel to Sharp Tor across the moors. There you will meet The Little Man in the Lantern. By the light of his lantern he will surely find a laugh.'

'Thank you m'lady and goodnight.'

Pasco dug his way out of the mole hill. He knew Sharp Tor was still in East Cornwall as the Lady Want had told him. Travelling across the moors in search of his laugh, Pasco came first to the village of Pensilva, then he walked across the moor to Minions and on higher into the moor until he came to the edge of a vast marsh. Pasco sniffed the wind for his lost laugh but all he felt was sadness. He began to cry. Then, first dimly and getting brighter, a light came gliding across the marsh. If it had been gliding away, perhaps Pasco would have followed the light into the deep marshes like many a hapless traveller before him. But the Little Lantern Man was gliding toward Pasco, amazed to see a piskey alone and crying on the edge of the marsh.

'Little Lantern Man with your bright light. Have you seen my lost laugh?' asked Pasco.

'There are no laughs around these lonely marshes, sad fellow. Come, climb into my lantern and travel in it to Dozmary Pool. There you can ask Tregeagle where he has seen it.'

'Tregeagle, the great spectre of Bodmin Moor. I shouldn't dare.'

'He travels all Cornwall, running away from the devil. He is sure to have found your laugh.'

Pasco climbed into the glimmering lantern and became a little light travelling across the moor. At Dozmary Pool, Pasco crept up to Tregeagle as he emptied a shell of water onto the already wet and marshy moor. 'Tregeagle, I have lost my laugh,' Pasco whispered.

'Lost your laugh? I have lost my soul,' wailed Tregeagle, blowing out the lantern. 'How dare you come to bemoan a lost laugh, little

Piskey, when you have no hope of retrieving my soul.' And Tregeagle wailed with a horrifying sadness that made poor Pasco feel even more solemn than before. Pasco ran away to hide in the rushes.

After what seemed to Pasco like forever, he heard the rumble of galloping hooves and a herd of wild horses carrying Piskey Night-Riders reined up at the pool to drink. Spying Pasco moping in the rushes, the Night-Riders hauled him onto one of their horses and galloped off into the night.

'Where are we going?' Pasco asked, when he dared.

'We are going on a galloping adventure to see all of Caradon,' said the piskey onto whose stiff red jacket Pasco clung.

And so they did. In no time it seemed, the Night-Riders were off the moor and galloping through West Taphouse, then on through Lerryn and Lansallos, where they paused for a moment to look out to sea and explore the pretty cove. Then in a flash they were racing along the coast path. The line of stolen horses seemed to know the route and the Piskey Night-Riders whooped in delight as they careered along the edge of the cliffs. They flew past Polperro and Looe, turning inland at Seaton.

'Where are we going now?' Pasco whimpered.

'On a quest up the Hessenford Valley,' sang the Night-Riders.

'And now?' Pasco asked as they leapt over hedges into fields.

'On a quest to Quethiock,' they sang, laughing all the way, to which Pasco could only bite his lip in shameful silence. Quethiock seemed no distance from the sea to these racing Night-Riders. No wonder the farmers found their horses piskey-ridden and foaming all over. As they travelled, they interrogated Pasco and Pasco sniffed a confession; he had lost his laugh.

'The last piskey we knew who lost his laugh was strung up in a sack and hung upside down like a mouse so no one could hear his misery,' the Night-Riders told Pasco gruffly.

Pasco felt more and more frightened at the thought of being strung in a sack, and seeing they were approaching the castle at Gelliwig, he slid off his mount and into a mound of freshly dug earth. Lady Want seemed to be prepared for him this time and she even had a better suggestion to find his laugh.

'Pasco, may I suggest King Arthur to advise you,' she said magnanimously.

And looking up from the dirt, Pasco saw a huge chough, a black bird with distinctive long red legs and a red beak, perched on a stunted tree beside them.

'Piskey,' said the chough. 'It is always a good idea to first look in the place you last had the item lost, and I believe yours was the fairy ring on my lawn.'

'The King speaks wisely,' agreed the mole.

And Pasco went gingerly over to the ring of soft tufted grass on the edge of Gelliwig. Sure enough, rolling about in a jumble of laughter was what could only have been the lost piskey laugh. Pasco threw himself at his laugh in delight and began to dance while laughing and laughing. The other piskeys soon joined him and they formed a ring with Pasco in it and danced and danced until the sun left the day.

TOWNS ON THE EDGE OF THE MOOR

8

CALLINGTON

'Hingston Down well wrought
is worth London Town, well bought.'

*Callington is a town surrounded by moors. Not far from the centre
of town, Bodmin Moor's Caradon Hill and Sharp Tor are visible,
as are nearby Kit Hill and not so far away the peaks of Dartmoor.
A mining town, Callington's buildings are granite grey but the spirit
of the town is bright. The Honey Fair takes place in October and is a
popular event attended by people for miles around. Callington May
Fair is constantly growing with workshops in Cornish music, dance
and song, and giant making. The lively procession of Callington
Giants culminates in a spectacular serpent dance that takes over the
town centre.*

*King Arthur's travelling court gathered every year for the spring
festival of Whitsun at Gelliwig-ton, later known as Callington.
The knights at court included Arthur's nephew, Caradoc. Born in
Brittany, the son of the King of Nantes, Caradoc came to Britain as
a child to Arthur's knight school. Later he became a celebrated local
knight and it is perhaps from him came the area name Caradon. The
Arthurian tales of Gelliwig are the tales of Caradoc's adventures, and
are over a thousand years old. They were originally sung by wandering minstrels, or jongleurs, and so here they are told in ballad form.*

The Challenge

Newly knighted Caradoc takes up a challenge from a stranger visiting court. He must behead the stranger, and then lay his own head on the block in a year's time.

King Arthur called upon his court,
to gather for feasting.
Whitsuntide at Gelliwig.
Fine times all were seeking.

He wished to knight Caradoc,
who came with fifty lads,
Arthur's spirit was generous,
'I'll knight them all – be glad!'

Guenevere dressed Caradoc,
in embroidered linen,
adjusted sword and mantle,
a fitting beginning.

Sir Gawain fixed on his right spur,
Yvain fixed his left.
Caradoc was knighted.
What would be his quest?

A great feast was all laid out,
and Arthur wished for jest.
A stranger rode up huge and fierce,
The King greeted his guest.

Arthur asked, 'Why are you here?'
Stranger: 'For a challenge.'
He swung aloft a gleaming sword,
'I seek bravery not talent.

I'll lay my head upon the block,
for the sword of a knight.'
The King said, 'A bit rash, don't you think?'
The Stranger, 'Just one smite

and in return a blow to the neck,
just one year from today.'
'We've no knight foolish enough.
Take the stranger away.'

'Arthur, all the land will learn,
your brave knights refused me.'
Caradoc rashly ran forward,
'I'm your man, I'll not flee.'

'Are you Arthur's bravest knight?
Rather, his biggest fool.'
The stranger's head was on the block,
'I know you'd rather duel.'

Caradoc took his sword and cut
off the head to laughter,
as it rolled across the ground,
the body ran right after.

The headless stranger spurted blood,
his spectacle gaudy.
Carefully he picked up his head,
put it on his body.

Stranger cried, 'I've surprised you,
I've survived the deed.
I'll return to take your head
as we've all agreed.'

At the thought of a beheading,
the court felt great unease,
they would reform at Whitsun time,
this year would be no breeze.

All too soon the year went by,
Caradoc to lose his head.
'I'll give you a ransom – anything!'
 King Arthur quickly said.

Caradoc saw the sword raised high,
this blade he couldn't flee.
Young Caradoc feared his death.
'Please, why don't you strike me?'

Stranger used the flat of his sword.
Caradoc's life not through.
Stranger told a secret,
'What I say you'll rue.

I'm your father and you're my son.
Come, I shall embrace you.'
In turn they all hugged Caradoc,
Asking him, 'Is this true?'

Caradoc sat with the stranger,
who was an Enchanter.
He'd thought he had a father,
But now he had another.

CARADOC GETS THE GIRL

Tegan and Cador's father, the High King of Cornwall, had recently died and they needed to claim his lands. Riding through the woods on the way to Arthur's court Gilliwig, they met Sir Alardin, who tried to woo Tegan but she refused him. Spurned, Alardin decided to take her anyway. Cador and Alardin fought, Cador was wounded and Alardin carried Tegan away. Sir Caradoc galloped up.

Cador was wounded, near death,
his sister was taken.
Slung over Alardin's horse,
her liberty shaken.

Riding toward Alardin,
was the knight Caradoc,
calling, 'Who hangs from your steed?
Riding freely? Now you mock.'

'I'll never give her to you,
I won her fair and square.'
'It's obvious you didn't.
Now fight me if you dare.'

Caradoc swung his sharp sword,
Alardin struck an arm,
the combat was fierce and violent,
both struggled in alarm.

Their shields and chainmail shredded,
Alardin in retreat,
his sword was quickly broken.
He admitted defeat,

'Tell me your name my conqueror,
I am at your service.'
'I'm Caradoc, Arthur's nephew.
Surrender in earnest.'

They hoisted Cador between them
and Alardin led on
to the Lady of the Pavillion,
she'd cure all that was wrong.

When treated they all feasted,
Caradoc made friendships,
felt a love for lady Tegan,
a love that was endless.

CARADOC BRIEFBRAS

*Some years after discovering his true father is an enchanter, Caradoc
goes home to Brittany. Here he confronts his parents as to the true
nature of his birth. His father is very angry and imprisons the queen
in a tower. She is enraged with Caradoc for airing her secret.*

Sir Caradoc left Cornwall.
Travelled all the way to France.
He had some distressing news
to give the King of Nantes.

'I'm sorry, King, to tell you,
that you are not my father.
My true father's an enchanter –
My Mother loved another.'

The King was really angry,
locked his queen away.
'She has been untrue to me,
the tower's where she'll stay.'

Furious, the false queen called
the enchanter to her tower.
'Our son is a traitor. Kill him.
My love for him is sour.'

Pleadingly, she flashed her eyes
playing to his weakness.

'Hide a snake in my wardrobe
I'm distraught I confess.'

Enchanter conjured up a snake.
It slithered into the dark.
'Tell our boy to fetch a comb.'
He wished he'd had no part.

'Caradoc dear, fetch my best comb.'
In he reached and gasped.
The snake curled right around his arm
so tight the pain grew vast.

Word travelled Sir Caradoc lay
dying of enchantment.
Cador sailed to Brittany,
his helpfulness granted.

Not wanting his friend to see his pain,
Caradoc hid his face.
He went to a hermitage,
a quiet, secluded place.

At last Cador found the hut,
where hid his dying friend.
'Why do you hide your face,
all alone at the end?'

Caradoc wept, telling his friend
the curse was his mother's.
Cador rode to the tower
hoping for a wonder.

Was the queen's son truly dead?
Or was he still alive?

Cador told her of Caradoc,
for his life she must strive.

The queen summoned the Enchanter,
whose long face looked grave,
'What is it you want now my Queen?
An end to this I crave.'

'Bold Enchanter, tell me
how, I might save my son.'
'Queen, a brave girl you must find,
for the spell to be undone.

She must prove she feels for him
a love as strong as silk.
Fill two tubs, far apart,
with vinegar and milk.

Let the milk bathed girl entice the snake
her naked form in view.
As the serpent leaps to greet her
a sword shall slice the snake in two.'

Cador returned to Cornwall
to bring back his brave sister.
Tegan would gladly risk her life,
relieved they did enlist her.

Caradoc looked hideous,
shrouded in cloak and hood.
'I tell you I would rather die
than risk dear Tegan for good.'

Cador persuaded Caradoc,
so they prepared the scene.
Tegan stood ready in the milk,
Cador in between.

Caradoc stepped into the vat
of the stinking vinegar.
Snake clung snugly on his arm.
Would it release its prisoner?

When the deadly snake leapt,
Cador stood sword in hand,
he sliced off the serpent's head,
freeing the deadly band.

Caradoc was now without the snake
but withered in his limb.
'We'll call you short in the arm,'
Tegan laughed with him.

Tegan's bravery had saved him,
I think we'll all agree.
'I'm hopeful for our future,
Tegan. Will you marry me?'

Caradoc Briefbras (short in the arm) married Tegan. They lived happily and he became King Caradoc and she Tegan, Queen of Cornwall.

THE MANTLE

Every year Arthur, the High King, came to Cornwall to hold court. One year, a magician arrived at the court with a magic mantle.

Maytime at Gelliwig
King Arthur was feasting
Knights and their ladies
enjoying the evening.

A stranger arrived
and waved his wand.
A mantle appeared
it shimmered and shone.

'When a lady is false
the mantle will curl
when her love is true
its silk will unfurl.'

The ladies came forward
to prove their loyalty
first was Guinevere
for she was royalty.

Arthur wrapped the mantle
about her shoulders fair
the mantle curled stiff
her false heart laid bare.

One by one the ladies
slipped beneath the mantle's mane
one by one the ladies
ran away in shame.

Next spoke Caradoc,
'My Tegan's surely true.
Try it on my darling,
see what it will do.'

Right round Tegan's shoulders
the shining cloak was draped
its silks rippled loose
the knights all agape.

Caradoc took Tegan
in a merry embrace
the mantle swirled free
enhancing her grace.

DUPATH WELL

Hingston Down once referred to the area east of Callington and included Kit Hill. It is an important place historically in Cornwall. In 838 a great battle took place across Hingston Down, a battle between the Cornish and the Vikings against the Saxons. The Saxons won and it was from this moment Cornwall became part of England. The area is rich in tin. In the Middle Ages, tin miners had their own laws and together with Devon men, held their stannary parliament at Kit Hill. South of Kit Hill, on a farm on the outskirts of Callington, is Dupath Well. A granite building, it was built in 1510 by the Augustan canons of St Germans Priory. It has a baptistry and oratory where visitors can pray and bathe in the holy water. The spring over which the well house is built is said to be a cure for whooping cough. Here is the tale of Dupath Well, a tale of medieval knights.

Sir Colan stood by Dupath Well, a full moon lit the dusky sky. The Lady Michelle watched him as he waited for his opponent. Sir Colan was everything to Lady Michelle and she felt she could never love another man. Standing beside her was her father, who had firmly chosen Gottlieb to marry Michelle. At last Gottlieb arrived, the night air hung fraught with expectation.

Gottlieb and Sir Colan launched into a bitter duel for the hand of Lady Michelle. Their duel took place beside a spring of healing water but this was not a night for healing. The battle was violent and bloody. The Lady cried out as Sir Colan was killed before her eyes. Her father held her arm steady and congratulated Gottlieb, who was soon to be his son-in-law. But Michelle was destined never to be married. Hours later, Gottlieb also died of his wounds and Lady Michelle vowed Sir Colan had been the only man for her.

9

LAUNCESTON AND SURROUNDINGS

'Don't you hear the fond tale of the sweet nightingale
as she sings in the valley below.'

*The town of Launceston is deep within farmland and surrounded by
tiny villages. Launceston Castle rises on a hill, high up above the town
and clearly visible on the approach. The castle green is open and free
to visit. Launceston was once the capital of Cornwall. It is set close to
the River Tamar and the Devon border, just off the A30 and easily
accessible as a first stop on a trip to Cornwall. Cornwall's finest poet,
Charles Causley, taught at the National School and lived at No. 2
Cypress Well. A rotating Poet in Residence lives and works there today
as part of the Charles Causley Trust. Walking around Launceston's
streets, beneath the shadow of the castle, there is a feeling of being
close to an ancient past. It would perhaps, not be surprising to meet
a pirate, playing a lute, coming around the corner. Taking the path
through the castle grounds, past the museum and on down the hill to
the right, you come to Dockacre Road leading back up to the centre
of town. On a sharp bend, running alongside the road, is the very old
Dockacre House.*

THE GHOST OF DOCKACRE

Elizabeth Herle lived at Dockacre House in Launceston. She was especially house-proud; everything in Dockacre House had its place and she kept strict order. One evening, Elizabeth was feeling pleased as she had made a delicious meal. All the town's dignitaries were coming to dinner and she was making a special effort. Launceston town had everything she needed for the supper and Elizabeth had spent a good part of the morning chatting in the market as she collected locally grown ingredients. It had taken her quite a while to walk through the castle and down the hill home. Going was slow as Launceston was full of the remains of animals, whale bones, elephant bones and a stag's head or two. Throughout the house, every detail had been taken care of, right down to the collection of walking sticks kept by the front door. The walking sticks at Dockacre House always stood in a particular order. On the right end of the row was a new stick, bought that very day by Elizabeth's husband Nicholas; it had a flute attached and looked very ornate.

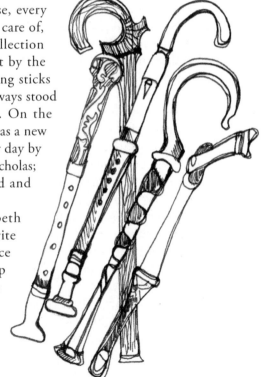

That night Elizabeth dressed in her favourite dress: a simple bodice with a skirt made up of layers and layers of baby pink silk. It was perhaps a little young for her – Elizabeth was aware of that, but the material was sumptuous and she felt so very pretty. Nicholas complimented her affably as she came down the stairs and stood at his side. They were the most handsome and well-liked couple Launceston had. Everyone had accepted their invitation and soon many footsteps arrived at the door. A particular friend of Nicholas, the town's up-and-coming banker, Thomas Williams, teased Nicholas about his new walking stick.

'What an extravagance, Herle. I bet it doesn't actually play.'

'Well of course it does. Play it for him, Nicholas,' Elizabeth demanded, bored with pleasantries.

With great care, Nicholas took the flute to his mouth and played *The Sweet Nightingale.*

'Full of surprises you are, Herle,' said Tommy, shaking his head and leading his wife into the dining room.

As all their guests had arrived, Nicholas and Elizabeth followed them, Nicholas feeling slightly abashed at his performance, as he didn't usually reveal his love of music. He and Tommy had spent most of their childhood out in the fields shooting. Tommy's father had turned a blind eye to them taking his gun bag as the two boys had always returned with something good for supper.

Elizabeth sat with her husband in the centre of the long, dark wooden table. They faced the door with their backs to an impressive stuffed stag's head. The stag had apparently been hunted on Bodmin Moor, although no one in living memory could remember where or when. Elizabeth watched the progress of the meal with a keen eye. Her two maids served it beautifully and everyone appeared to be enjoying the food. Elizabeth began to relax and enjoy the evening herself. She knew Tommy and Nicholas were drinking more than was acceptable but no one seemed to have noticed; rather the majority of her guests were enjoying their drink as much as their food.

After a time, Elizabeth began to fret, her precise control of events was slipping. She got up and began to circle the table making sure the desserts were to everyone's liking. So engrossed was Elizabeth in her attention to detail, she didn't notice her husband and Tommy leaving the room and not until too late did she see them return. Elizabeth had been wiping a dollop of cream off a chair, her head concealed by the tablecloth. As she stood up, she heard a shot and felt the pain searing into her very being. In her last moments, Elizabeth Herle looked her husband in the eyes and wondered, *did he shoot me on purpose?*

Nicholas Herle stood frozen with shock, staring at the stag's head. He was usually a much better aim. Tommy's bullet had sunk into the stag; Nicholas' bullet lay embedded in his wife. He made himself walk slowly around the table, he gathered the blooded, baby pink silk about Elizabeth and carried her upstairs out of sight.

Ever since the night of Elizabeth Herle's death, the people of Launceston have debated it. Did her husband kill her and, if so, what was his motive? Did the entire dinner party shoot her as she stood before the stag? Finally, was her murder a terrible accident, or had it been meticulously planned? If so, it would be worth remembering Nicholas played the flute on his new walking stick the night his wife died. Legend has it, whenever an occupant of Dockacre House has played the fluted walking stick, a member of their family has died soon afterward. Elizabeth Herle's ghost is thought to haunt Dockacre House. To this day, there have been many instances of objects being moved back into an exact position, doors opening and if the walking sticks by the front door are not left in order, they rattle through the night, rearranging of their own accord.

DIGORY PIPER

Five and a half miles from Launceston is Piper's Pool, a hamlet consisting of small bungalows, a Methodist chapel, and farms and houses hugging the winding roads to Bude and Egloskerry. The sound of traffic mingles with birdsong, dogs barking and a hum of bees. A wind farm does its work in neighbouring fields. The hedges are dense with trees and farmland spreads to the horizon. The tale from Piper's Pool is about a real person, Digory Piper, the World's Worst Pirate.

Name's Captain Digory Piper, pirate. Born at Piper's Pool, Launceston. One lucky day, myself and my partner, Richard Hodges, were given a privateer's licence to attack Spanish ships by the judge of the Admiralty, one Julius Caesar. Us and our ship the *Sweepstake*, were to sail off on the high seas to take the galleon's goods and merchandise belonging to the King of Spain. We were not to take the ships of our Queen Elizabeth's friends. Every Spanish ship had to be taken to the nearest port and a list made of everything and the value added up. The thing was, I didn't like rough seas; I liked calm seas where I could relax and play my lute. Instead of sailing over the high seas tracking Spanish galleons, I sailed up and down the English Channel, looting every ship I saw. We attacked French, Flemish and Danish boats and took all the treasure into Cornwall.

'Spect you've heard the grand tales of Frances Drake. He's a pirate same as me but his adventures are admired whereas mine come to nothing. For Drake it all goes right. They say he even took water to Plymouth. That's right, I'll tell you about it.

The people of Plymouth had very little water; they had to send their clothes to Plympton to be washed. Frances Drake was proud of Plymouth and promised everybody he would sort out the inconvenience. He rode into Dartmoor and found a spring. He whacked his horse's side and said some magical words. The horse galloped off and the water followed Drake all the way to Plymouth.

Now look at that galleon, a foreign one as well. We'll plunder it for what we can and take the spoils back to Cornish shores. Cases of gold coins, handsome. Jewels, chests of gold and silver, barrels of brandy and wine and food; everything Launceston could wish for. Everything good you can think of they will have on that ship for me to take home. Now, I've been told to give my takings to the Queen Elizabeth on reaching shore. Why would I want to do that? What is mine is mine and like I said, this Danish ship has everything could keep a man happy. Aye aye, my hearties.

I know, I know she's not a Spanish ship. I never saw a Spanish ship on the Channel to be honest. I've been thinking of a good way to sink the Spanish galleons without them expecting, that is when I do come across one. I'd get myself a good tree trunk and chop it into blocks with my hatchet. I'd set each block on fire and throw them into the sea and they would come up a fire block and sail right into the galleons before they even noticed. I could have a whole fleet of burning Spanish ships before they were the wiser. I would be Sir Digory Piper, our queen's hero.

As it is, Drake is seen as a hero by our Queen Elizabeth, for sinking the right ships. I'm not long for this world for sinking all the wrong ones. Not that it matters, I've had a time of it. Not everything went right for Drake, mind. Drake's wife nearly married another chap right in the middle of Plymouth. Drake had been abroad for years and his wife thought him dead. She thought she was free to marry another man she had grown fond of and the church was fixed. It happened Drake was at the opposite end of Devon and his spies told him he was about to lose his wife. He got up and fired one of his great guns so that it fired right across the county and into the church, exploded and fell between his lady and her intended. Of course, she then knew he was alive and the wedding was abandoned. They say Drake 'shot the gulf' when he sailed through the Magellan Strait on his first voyage. He used his pistol to shoot the gulf. Well I never heard anything so ridiculous. I expect he just kept sailing after the Spanish and found himself on the other side of the world.

I did have some luck in the end. Although I was sent to the justice of the Admiralty to be tried for sinking the Danish ship, I kept my life, which is more than can be said for most. Had to pay back what I'd taken, which was a little on the difficult side, seeing as I had given it all away. Took up busking with my lute on the streets of Launceston; not what you would expect from a pirate but locals seemed to enjoy it.

BETSY LAUNDRY

On the eastern edge of Bodmin Moor is North Hill, situated between Minions and Launceston. North Hill is surrounded by fields and the River Lynher flows through its farmland. North Hill has a church, a holy well of St Torney and the parish has four farms. In the days before free doctors and the NHS, every village had a witch, providing healing herbal remedies and charms. A lucky village had a good witch who could nearly always help her villagers. North Hill's witch was called Betsy Laundry.

North Hill's folklore collector was Barbara Spooner. Originally from Surrey, she came to live in Cornwall when she was 30 in 1923 and was a founding member of the North Hill Old Cornwall Society. Barbara travelled widely on foot over Bodmin Moor collecting tales and fragments of folklore, which she published in Old Cornwall, *the journal of the Old Cornwall Society. She was made a bard of the Gorsedd in 1930; her bardic name was Myrgh An Hallow (Daughter of the Moors). Barbara preserved Betsy's memory.*

Betsy Laundry was a witch. Not a fire starting, oath spitting, vexing kind of a witch; Betsy's charms cured ills, Betsy's spells righted wrongs and she was a useful member of the community. Betsy had lived in her cottage in North Hill for as long as anyone could remember. One day, Betsy bent down to take a tray with a pasty out of the range. She put the pasty on the table set for one and went back to put on another log. After eating a corner of her supper, she crept onto her knees and lifted a slab of hard, ragged stone slates from her kitchen floor. She lifted the slate floor each day to check on her companions; the five toads who were crouching in the cool darkness underneath. Then this morning, as every morning, Betsy went out to look in amongst the ditches for toads for her collection.

She walked across the field to the River Lynher. It was a rainy day, a mist hung over the fields and the river and the water was black. Betsy folded her equally black hair over her shoulder and scrabbled about in the marsh by the river, searching. There was a lot of different birdsong so Betsy had stopped her scavenging to listen and she hadn't heard a boy and a girl come up behind her. The boy was crying and the girl was pushing him forward to talk to Betsy. 'It's my brother, he's afeard of you but he has an awful nettle sting and we were hoping you might help,' said the girl.

'That I can do something about,' said Betsy, her skirt half an inch thick with mud. 'Come here.' Betsy scrabbled about some more, looking for something on the edge of the field. She held up a dock leaf to the sting and said,

    'Out nettle, in dock:
    Dock shall have a new smock.'

The boy gaped at Betsy because the nettle sting had gone. 'Thanks,' he said.

'Now, I expect you'll be wanting to see my toads,' said Betsy.

The two children followed Betsy across the field and into her cold kitchen.

'Fire has gone out, I've been out the kitchen too long,' Betsy said.

The children huddled together and watched as Betsy carefully moved the slab. Five toads sat hunched in the earth, their black eyes watched the children. 'I expect you'll be wanting to hear why I'm keeping them? Well, I'll tell you and just you two, in all these years. Long ago, witches like me weren't accepted as part of North Hill village, or anywhere else for the matter. Every witch was hunted and tried at Launceston. Most were seen to lose their lives but I'm telling you, they didn't, not entirely. Their bodies all disappeared and their voices too but something was left behind. All those years ago, my job was to turn the witches into toads just before they were due to die. Trouble was, I never found the toads very easily. I tried to follow them as they scurried away but I wasn't always successful what with all the crowds gathered around. Every day, I go out looking and some days I find one. The toads are very good at charms and they are the reason I have continued to live for all these years.'

Betsy Laundry led the children out into her garden, then went back the kitchen. She slipped the sixth toad out of her skirts in with the others and shut the lid.

BODMIN
AND BEYOND

10

GOSS MOOR, BODMIN AND FOWEY

'Into Bodmin and out of this World.'

Travelling into Cornwall, stories are of saints and ancient kings.

Castle an Dinas has Bronze Age barrows and an Iron Age hill fort. It is located a mile north off the A30 at Goss Moor, not far from St Columb Major. The hill fort is centrally inland. Standing on its grassy heights, you can see an incredible panoramic view of Cornwall. The north coast and the sea at Newquay are clearly in view, as are Rough Tor and Brown Willy, Roche Rock and the Clay Country. Long ago, people would have felt incredibly secure; they could see enemy horses coming and camp fires smoking. Castle an Dinas has three ditches and embankments circling its slopes. It was the site of Cornwall's largest Wolfram mine.

Close by is Goss Moor, a National Nature Reserve, managed by Natural England. It is mostly heathland and scrub, a watery moor — wetland with many bogs, streams and pools. Cattle are grazed freely here, with ponies, sheep and cows to be seen sheltering their young. Tin was mined on the moors between the eleventh and nineteenth centuries. Now in contrast to its mining past, Goss Moor is habitat to many rare plants, butterflies and moths. Circling Goss Moor is a 7-mile cycle track with a purpose-laid surface suitable for all to use.

Long ago, Castle an Dinas was King Arthur's hunting seat. When he came to the moor to hunt wild boar, King Arthur's horse stamped on a moor stone, leaving the prints of his hooves in rock. Although the hoofed stone is now long lost in memory, it is held as proof Arthur came to hunt at Goss Moor. Once a great battle took place at the castle and all over Goss Moor. It was the battle in which Arthur fought Mordred and the rebels. Mists came down over the moors and the fighters and no one could see whether they were maiming friend or foe. Something else proves King Arthur was at Goss Moor and Castle an Dinas – the distant sound of battle etched in the moorland winds.

THE PISKEY WARRIORS

Eight-year-old Jory Williams was cycling along the cycle trail at Goss Moor. Coming to the end of the track, he turned left onto the old A30. A mile along the road, Jory felt mazed. Where was he exactly? He saw another track on the opposite side of the road and decided to take a look. He cycled up the bumpy, rugged track until he came onto a circular, grassy path leading around Castle an Dinas. Jory was very pleased to have found it all by himself and he very much wanted to walk up through the outer rings to the top of the hill fort. Having cycled way ahead of his mum, dad and his baby sister, he had a bit of time before they caught up and Jory thought he would explore the fort. Leaving his bike by the side of the trail, he set out.

All of a sudden, a thick fog swept across the moors. Jory could smell the fog before he saw it whisking all about him. He turned back, thinking he could get away to his bike but he wasn't entirely sure which direction to take. Who knew where he would stray

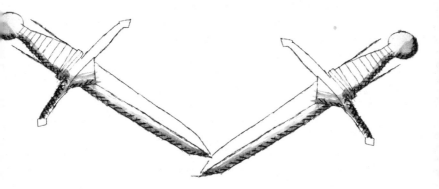

to if he left for his bike, hardly able to see the end of his nose? Instead, Jory got down onto his hands and knees and methodically felt his way across the grass, moving slowly forward until he felt the outer wall of the castle rampart. Jory stumbled over the mound and into a ditch of ferns and waited for the fog to lift.

Lying alone in the arms of the ancient hill fort, Jory listened for the sound of his parents coming to help him. At first, he thought it was the bark of a moorland cow. He listened more closely and was sure he heard the cries of soldiers fighting all about him. Could it really be a battle was taking place in the fog? This was a castle after all and castles were meant to be full of knights and fights. Jory lay back and listened to the baying and snorting of horses, the clash of swords and shields, the shouts of pain and command. He imagined he himself had command of this battle, like he did when he played with his wooden fort in his bedroom. Shouting along with the battle and enjoying himself immensely, Jory was not at all surprised when figures began to emerge from the fog. They were not the huge muscled knights of King Arthur's hunt as he expected. Instead two handsome armies of the little people fought a mighty battle in the fog at Castle an Dinas. The piskey warriors were all dressed in red jackets with green hats and they were excellent riders of tiny moorland horses. They fought a long and bloody battle, their shouts thick in the air. Jory watched the piskey armies for what felt like forever and he forgot all about being stranded on the moor in the fog.

As suddenly as its arrival, the fog lifted and with it the piskey warriors vanished. Jory lay stunned by what he had witnessed.

'That was awesome,' he said to himself.

He looked all about him for signs of battle; a broken sword, a maimed piskey, piles of bloody bodies. The castle was just as he had found it. The mists and fog and the piskey warriors had all well and truly vanished. After a time, Jory brushed himself off and walked back to his bike. He found it easily, as standing by it were his mum and dad and baby sister.

Jory has not forgotten his trip to Goss Moor and Castle an Dinas or the piskey warriors. He has succeeded in persuading his parents to take him on the cycle trail many times since. On every trip to Goss Moor, one of his parents has made sure they ride ahead with him and although he will never stop hoping, Jory has not yet seen the piskey warriors again.

PETROC AND THE MONSTROUS DRAGON

St Petroc came to Cornwall with a mission to convert everybody to Christianity. He landed at Trebetherick on the river Camel and founded a monastery at Lanwethinoc (Padstow). Sometimes he felt sociable and joined the monastery; other times he went off to be alone as a hermit. One day, Petroc met the warrior Prince Constantine out hunting deer. Petroc called for the huntsmen to call off his dogs as the deer was under Petroc's protection. Constantine laughed and raised his sword. Petroc looked the prince in the eye and paralysed him. As the prince shouted to be freed, Petroc stood calmly and said he would only free him if Constantine became a Christian. Constantine joined the monastery at Padstow and built his own church at what is now known as Constantine Bay. He lived in prayer under St Petroc's guidance for the rest of his life. St Petroc also founded a priory at Bodmin, which became very popular amongst monks and pilgrims. Again, the priory was so busy, Petroc would often take himself off to spend time as a hermit.

Bodmin is home to Bodmin and Wenford Steam Railway, connecting Bodmin to the main line at Bodmin Parkway. Bodmin town has been working toward being pedestrianised. It is a centre for cycling; the Camel Trail begins at Bodmin and cyclists can take the trail to Wadebridge and then on to Padstow, a beautiful ride alongside the river estuary. Petroc and his monks would no doubt have travelled between the priories by bicycle if living today. The ruins of Bodmin Priory are to the left of the roundabout on the entrance to the town opposite St Petroc's Church. Inside the church is a font with an ornate carving of a serpent, the very monstrous dragon encountered by St Petroc in the following tale.

St Petroc lived his life by values of love, kindness, forgiveness, loyalty and faith. A solver of problems and a miracle worker, Petroc was happy to help both people and animals. He gathered about him a group of monks and together they built a new priory in Bodmin. Petroc found himself establishing his life as a hermit on the one hand and a leader of monks on the other. One day, as he was praying quietly, much commotion and screams of terror came from the fields and woods nearby. Petroc sent word to find out what or who was disturbing his prayers. It was not long before he received an answer.

The people of Bodmin told the tale of an evil man who kept a pit of snakes to terrorise all living nearby. Criminals, and anyone who disobeyed the evil man, were punished by being thrown into the pit. Not long ago, the evil man had died and his son thought the pit a disgusting means of punishment. The son left the snakes in the pit to starve. They fought and ate one another until only the three strongest remained. These three snakes fought a great battle until only one snake was left alive. The last snake lay huge and swollen at the bottom of the pit. Its body no longer wriggled as a snake; it writhed and roared as a monstrous dragon.

The monstrous dragon climbed out of the snake pit and ate everything; it ate all the cattle in the farm next door, it ate the farmer and the farmer's dog. The monstrous dragon travelled all around Bodmin terrifying everyone and the people were most surprised Petroc hadn't been eaten.

'I have been deep in prayer,' said St Petroc. 'I must ask my friends Samson and Abbot Wethnoc to accompany me. We shall create together a shield of absolution and hope to defeat the dragon.'

The dragon stood eating, blocking the track. Petroc, Samson and Wethnoc walked toward the monstrous dragon. It stopped eating but, not wanting to leave its food, the beast hesitated. In an instant Petroc threw forward a heavenly shield. The saint took out a fresh handkerchief and walked toward the dragon's ghastly jaws. He wrapped the handkerchief around the jaws, hiding the worst and hoping to curb the people's terror, and he led the dragon away to the sea. Samson and Wethnoc followed, praying with all their being that St Petroc could keep the dragon tame.

On the way to the sea, St Petroc and the dragon were met by a party of mourners. The group of men were exhausted and weak. Between them they carried a dead young man. On seeing the monstrous dragon, the men all lay down in terror. Petroc stopped walking and stood quietly; the dragon followed his lead. Through prayers Petroc renewed the strength of the group of men. The dead man sat up, his life restored. The men celebrated by dancing and singing songs. They didn't notice St Petroc and the dragon slip away to the sea. There, Petroc asked the dragon to promise never to harm human or animal again. The dragon prostrated itself before St Petroc in agreement and swam off to live deep under the sea and was never seen in Bodmin again.

TRISTAN AND ISOLDE

The River Fowey rises on Bodmin Moor and flows through the Glynn Valley and on to Lostwithiel and Fowey, where it meets the sea. Fowey Harbour is one of the largest and deepest on the Cornish coast and is able to take huge ships. The river is a dank green and scores of boats bob on a choppy water. The Fowey River boats are grouped with a rainbow of brightly coloured covers. Opposite Fowey is Polruan; the Bodinnick Ferry connects Fowey and Polruan. RNLI have a large lifeboat moored at Fowey and there are tankers in the river. Fowey is a lovely town to visit with interesting independent shops including a friendly bookshop. There are pubs and cafes alongside the river, and many water sports to be tried. Fowey gives the impression of having a slow, relaxed way of life in and out of the river.

By the side of the road on the approach to Fowey is the Tristan Stone. It has been moved several times, originating at nearby Castle Dore. The 8ft stone is fifth century with a sixth century Latin inscription, GRVSTANS HIC IACIT CVNOWORI FILIUS, translated as 'Trystan here lies of Cunomorus the son'. The writing on the granite is no longer visible – here, history is fading. From Castle Dore, a vast

*panorama of land can be seen and a section of the River Fowey. An
earthen hill fort, Castle Dore, has a larger oval rampart without and
a circular rampart within. There is a good ditch to the inner rampart
and a ditch on one side of the outer.*

Castle Dore was noisy but warm. The great wooden hall and many
roundhouses were built inside strong defences. The houses smelt of
animals as the pigs and hens had been brought inside due to persis-
tent Cornish rain. The hall smelt of sweet herbs, fresh straw, meat
and feasting, and it was home to Mark, King of Cornwall. King
Mark entertained many visitors as close by was a busy harbour.
A strong, thickset man of average height with long, dark curling
hair and beard, Mark was warm and kind. Many a lady had hoped
to marry him but he had not yet chosen a wife.

Tristan was the son of Rivalen, King of Lyonesse. His mother,
Isobel was the sister of Cornwall's King Mark. Sadly, Tristan's
mother died shortly after he was born and his father died in battle.

Baby Tristan was taken from Lyonesse to the safety of Castle Dore. Here, he was brought up by his uncle King Mark, and they became very close. Tristan grew to be handsome with long black hair and sea blue eyes. He had grown athletic through horse riding and fighting. Quiet with a steely determination, Tristan overcame all his adversaries. He modelled himself on Mark and would never have dreamed of betraying his trust. He was trained to be a knight and sent on many missions by his uncle.

One day, a ship arrived and moored in the harbour. Morholt of Ireland climbed up the hill to Castle Dore and asked to speak with the King of Cornwall. Seats were found for him and his men around the low table and food was bought out from the kitchen. Mark felt a wave of unease; the man he entertained was a feared and ruthless knight. When the visitors had eaten their fill, Morholt got down to business.

'I have come to claim the tribute you owe to the King of Ireland. Three hundred Cornish maids and youths will be chosen.'

'That is an impossible amount,' said Mark. 'Imagine my land full of weeping families.'

'Or,' said Morholt grimacing, 'Do you have a volunteer who dares sail to Ireland to fight me?'

Tristan stood up. 'I will fight you Morholt,' he said sternly. 'I am not afraid.'

King Mark had grave misgivings but had to let Tristan honour his promise. He would send Tristan away to Ireland.

'I accept the challenge,' King Mark said sadly.

Some days later, Tristan and Mark left Castle Dore together and walked down to the river mouth, where Tristan's boat swayed in the salty river. King Mark insisted Tristan sit with him for a tankard of mead, fearing these might be their last moments together. They watched the comings and goings as boats glided in, fish heaped in baskets their bellies gleaming a watery glow. The rowers on Tristran's boat laughed and joked. Mark was unusually silent, nervously sipping his drink. Tristran tried to reassure his uncle he would soon return and all would be resolved. When they were done, Tristan sailed away to Ireland to fight Morholt.

Morholt oozed confidence. He terrified every knight who came against him with his reputation for ruthless combat. Sitting calmly on his horse, Tristan knew this was to be the fight of his life. After much sparring and circling, Tristan watched as Morholt played to the cheering Irish crowd, showing off his huge athletic build. Morholt wasn't concentrating fully on the fight with Tristan. At the next clash of swords, Tristan easily stopped Morholt's blow with his shield and reached with all his strength as he brought his sword down into Morholt's helmet. So strong was the force of the blow, Morholt died instantly. A shard of Tristan's sword broke off and was left in the helmet. Tristan became a celebrated knight and the local people asked him to fight a dragon that had been terrorising the neighbourhood. He killed the dragon but in doing so was wounded. Bleeding and weak, Tristan was carried to the nearby castle and the queen gave the task of healing to her beautiful daughter, who was called Isolde.

Princess Isolde had a gift of healing and after a time, Tristan found himself revived and recovered. He sent word to King Mark, telling him of the astounding powers of Princess Isolde. King Mark replied with an offer of marriage to Isolde. Their marriage would make a strong alliance with Ireland and if the princess had the gift of healing, all the better. The queen was flattered the King of Cornwall should want to marry her daughter and accepted the offer at once on her daughter's behalf. She summoned Isolde to tell her of the marriage proposal. Isolde entered with her beautiful face downcast. She held up the helmet of her beloved uncle Morholt, drew out the broken shard and fitted it to Tristan's sword, which lent against her mother's throne.

'I cannot marry King Mark, knowing Tristan killed my uncle.'

'You will have to, my child. It has already been arranged.'

Fearing her daughter would extend her hatred for Tristan to his king, the queen made up a strong love potion. She instructed Isolde to share it with King Mark, telling her it would give them good health.

Tristan and Isolde prepared to sail for Cornwall. The voyage was rough and Isolde felt she needed a remedy. Tristan himself was white as surf. Relenting a little, Isolde wondered how she could help him.

'Come Tristan, we will share my mother's potion. Perhaps it will be a cure for sea sickness.'

Tristan gladly glugged down his share of the potion. And how interchangeable are love and hate. In an instant, Tristan and Isolde fell deeply in love. Rain came down hard and there was no wind. Tristan's men began to row. It would be a long journey home. Soaking wet and cold, Tristan and Isolde clung to one another all the way to Cornwall.

From the moment King Mark set eyes on Isolde, he fell in love with her also and knew he had chosen well, a beautiful bride. They were to be married quickly. This sent Mark into a whirl of preparations and Isolde to her room to ready herself. Being so busy, his head full of plans for married life, King Mark failed to notice the romantic connection between Tristan and Isolde. It became evident soon enough as the young lovers spent every minute they could steal together. They met on the cliff tops, hidden within secluded coves and anywhere they could find in the wooded valleys all about Castle Dore. As Queen Isolde always had her ladies in waiting with her, it was they who betrayed her infidelity to the king.

King Mark was desperately sad Tristan had betrayed him. However, he wasted no time in arranging for Tristan to marry another Isolde; Isolde of the White Hands. Mark sent Tristan away in his boat once more, to live across the sea with his new wife in Brittany. Promising his uncle he would forevermore relinquish his affection for Irish Isolde, Tristan sailed away. Watching him go, Isolde stood on the quay. She waved to Tristan with a huge white handkerchief. Isolde hid her face in the cloth as she convulsed with tears as Tristan's boat sailed for Brittany to meet his intended.

For years Tristan lived in Brittany with his new wife. He fought many battles and became a celebrated knight on a new shore. Isolde of the White Hands was very pretty but she was cold in her heart and did not have the passion to love and to heal possessed by Isolde of Ireland. One day, Tristan became injured fighting in Brittany. Tristan was desperately unwell. Nothing would cure him and Isolde was beside herself as to what to do.

'Tristan, is there anything at all that will give you strength?'

'There is.'

'Then I will do it, anything.'

'Send for Cornwall to Queen Isolde. She will heal me if anyone can.'

'As you wish.'

'Ask the ship to sail a white sail if Isolde is on board and a black sail if she is not.'

Tristan kept himself alive waiting for Isolde. He imagined her kindness and the strength of their love bound ever tighter over the years they had lived apart. Isolde was everything to him; he knew that now, had always known. If she came, he would forsake his friendship with Mark and take her away into the world so they might live together. Some of these musings he muttered as he slept. Isolde of the White Hand heard her husband utter his undying love for another woman and felt a searing rage.

'Isolde, can you see the ship?' Tristan asked. 'Is its sail black or white?'

'Tristan, I am sorry, the sail is black.'

Isolde of the White Hands stood by Tristan's bed and wrung her hands as she simultaneously watched his condition deteriorate and a boat with a white sail approach. Her face grew thunderous as she realised Tristan was dying because he had lost hope in his heart for the eternal love of Queen Isolde.

As Queen Isolde alighted the boat and walked to Tristan's bedchamber, she knew it was too late. Banishing his heartless, jealous wife, Queen Isolde gathered Tristan's limp body up into her arms and cried. Never again would they embrace on the cliffs of Cornwall linked by a magical love. Isolde cried for the loss of Tristan, the truest love she would ever know.

Queen Isolde sailed back to Cornwall, bringing Tristan's body with her. She had a large granite memorial placed on his grave beside Castle Dore. Isolde never recovered from her grief. She spent hours sitting beside the tall granite stone, looking out over the woods toward the river. The sky was dark with rumbling clouds, the trees a haze of dusky green. Isolde sat dreaming, remembering their time as young lovers when she first came to Cornwall. As a bright sun set over autumn harbour waters, Queen Isolde died of a broken heart. King Mark dug deep within himself, finding the strength to forgive his nephew and his wife. He buried Isolde by Tristan's side beneath the Tristan stone. Two briars grew before the stone, their blooms red as hearts, their stems entwining.

Tales from North Cornwall's Moors

11

BODMIN MOOR: THE HIGH MOOR

'See saw, Margery Daw,
Sold her bed and lay on the straw,
Sold her straw, and lay on hay,
Piskies came, and took her away.'

Just south of Camelford can be found the high moor, with its crowning tors, Rough Tor and Brown Willy (Cornish: Bron Wennili, 'hill of swallows'). Swathes of reeds and grasses adorn the slopes. At times tinted gold in the sun, then in a moment cloaked in dark shadows as clouds merge above the moor. A well walked grassy path leads up to Rough Tor, edged with reeds and peat bog, with evidence of many moorland animals. Climbing higher and looking back toward the sea, moorland seamlessly morphs into farmland and the north coast becomes visible. Just over the top of Rough Tor is the open moor, stretching across a vast valley and up toward Cornwall's highest point, Brown Willy. A wild horse and her foal stand close to the top of Little Rough Tor, balancing hooves on granite. Yellow flowers dot the grasses and high up, yellow mushrooms grow between the rocks. Peat bog lies black against bright green grass and muddy water. Patches of reeds grow out of cracks in granite. The sounds of birds and animals carry on the wind. A herd of cows runs across the moors, followed by a lone farmer riding a sturdy horse, perhaps just perhaps, she has piskeys riding in her mane.

PISKEYS ON THE MARE'S NECK

This is a story of the moors of North Cornwall, a place where piskeys play in their droves on the granite peaks of Rough Tor (pronounced row to rhyme with bow) and Brown Willy (Bron Wenilli), and shine their lanterns in the marshlands.

One evening, Josey Tregaskis was riding across the moors on his way home from Camelford market. Josey Tregaskis was a young farmer who had always loved horses and had found the mare he was riding as a filly out on this very moor. The mare always trotted across her field to nuzzle farmer Tregaskis. She was as fond of him as he was of she.

The mare trotted on and Josey rode with the rhythm of the moors. He could smell the horse and felt for the right grip with his thighs. The journey home was a treat to him. However tired he felt, the mare gave him a new energy. He would be home in no time. As they rode through the moors, the mare became more and more excitable; she jumped and skittered at every sound. The wind was, unusually, only a breeze. With no other riders in sight, and Farmer Tregaskis wondered what could be upsetting her.

Then he saw them – three piskeys clinging to her mane. They swung about, gripping with their hands and knees as they climbed up the mane. Farmer Tregaskis tried his best to ignore the extra riders. He shook his hair, and blinked his eyes, unsure whether he was imagining things but when he looked again, the piskeys were still there, busy on the mare's neck.

On his way to market, Farmer Tregaskis had listened to the birds singing from their nests in the moorland grasses. Now he heard tinkling laughter as the piskeys enjoyed the thrill of the ride on the mare's flapping mane. He tried his best to stay in the saddle as the mare broke into a gallop; she was eager to unseat the piskeys and get home. She stopped jumping and got herself into a fast rhythm, her hooves skilfully avoiding the granite clitter littering the moor. She rode fast up a tor and Farmer Tregaskis gulped with fear as she plunged down the other side, streaking through the bracken, dodging sheep and clumps of gorse.

Farmer Tregaskis opened his eyes when the motion stopped and he knew he was safely back at his farm. He slid off the mare's back and went to hold her head. She tossed it, showing him something: there, plaited into her mane, were tens of tiny stirrups ready for a whole fleet of piskeys to ride her across the moors. Farmer Tregaskis patted the mare's neck and she rested her head protectively on his shoulder. He knew she had done well not to unseat him and run away with the piskey riders; running wild and free as she had when she was as a young filly, before Farmer Tregaskis found her.

The Boy Who Played with the Piskeys

There was once a boy called Daniel who lived with his mother on the moor. They lived in a sparkling clean cottage. Daniel's mother was a very busy woman, the type who swept up the dust as soon as it fell. She was so busy taking jobs to keep them in food, gathering peat for the fire and cooking, there was no time left for Daniel. Of course, she chatted to him but she had no time to play, and a playmate Daniel longed for more than anything.

As the days grew longer and summer stretched its limbs along the moors, Daniel began to stay out later and roam further every day. He found lots of secret dips and soft grassy hillocks to lie about in and he had fun getting wet and muddy in the bog and laughing as he was tickled by the reeds. Daniel lay in the grasses watching the nesting birds. He saw foals' births and sheep taken ill. He froze in the wind and grew bronze in the sun. Life on the moor was seldom boring for Daniel but it was always just him and his experiences; he had no one to share them with. Until one morning, Daniel was playing by the bog not far from home, when he heard laughter. The laughter came from all about him and of a sudden he saw a ring of piskeys dancing on the heather. He lay in the grass watching the piskeys for a long time until they had forgotten their dance and began playing a game. More than anything in the world, Daniel wanted to join the piskeys. If only he could just for a moment, it would be so much fun to be part of a game. Without realising, Daniel edged closer until he was sitting in plain sight. One of the piskeys turned to wave at Daniel and another beckoned for him to join them. To his great surprise Daniel wasn't shy at all and he was soon standing in the middle of a piskey ring. All at once the piskeys took off their little green hats and threw them in the air in welcome. The piskey game was easy to pick up and Daniel found he was enjoying himself immensely.

When he grew tired, he went back to his seat and watched them until dark clouds began to roll over the moors. Daniel's mother would soon be calling him for supper and Daniel knew

he had best go home. But before he could be on his way, he found himself once more in the middle of a piskey ring. A piskey stepped forward and spoke to Daniel in a stern voice.

'You mustn't tell your mother you have played with piskeys. If you do tell her, we will never let you play with us again. If you keep quiet you can come to play with us every day.'

'I won't say a thing,' said Daniel confidently. His mother had never before asked him what he'd been doing and anyway, the answer would always be the same; out playing on the moor.

For many days, Daniel had the time of his life playing with the piskeys. They knew lots of games and always included Daniel, guiding him with much laughter. The moors will never ever be lonely again, Daniel thought to himself. I have friends, lots of friends.

But piskey friendship, like piskey kindness, is not necessarily forever. One day, Daniel was having so much fun he failed to notice the darkening of the sky and carried on with his piskey game.

Daniel's mother had dinner ready but Daniel was nowhere to be seen. Although he was always out and about during the day, Daniel was also always home for his dinner. Daniel's mother left the dinner keeping warm in the warming oven, hung her shawl about her shoulders and hastened up onto the moors to find her son. As she neared the place where the piskeys played, she thought she could hear laughter coming from all around her. She called to Daniel and he came running up the bank from the marsh.

'I'm just coming, Mother. Sorry I'm late,' he cried.

'You get yourself home as fast as you can.'

Daniel walked slowly home with his mother and ate his tea in silence. At last his mother spoke.

'Who were you playing with up on the moors? I could hear laughter but I couldn't see anyone.'

Daniel said nothing but his mother kept persisting. 'Come on, Daniel, you can tell me. A boy must tell his mother who his play-fellows are and, in any case, they must be strangers because we are the only family out on this part of the moor.'

In a very small voice Daniel said, 'They told me not to tell you.'

'Well, all the more reason I must know, Daniel.'

'I don't want to tell you because they said they would never play with me again.'

Daniel and his mother were quiet a while as they finished their tea and then as they sat in silence with their empty plates, Daniel realised he would have to tell her.

'I was playing with piskeys.'

'Piskeys?' she asked.

'Yes, Mother. I was terribly lonely and longed for someone to play with.'

'I am so sorry, Daniel. I will make time to play. We will explore the moors together; you will never be lonely again, I will make sure of it.' She gave him a big hug and went to find some sugar biscuits for pudding.

Daniel never did play with the piskeys again. He missed their games and merry laughter, but he was very happy his mother had time for him and they had many an adventure together.

The piskey tales set on the moors of North Cornwall were collected by Padstow's foremost literary lady, Nelly Sloggett, whose pen name was Enys Tregarthen. Nelly was born in 1850 in Padstow. Her father was a sailor and when he died, her mother worked as a charwoman. In 1867 at the age of 16, Nelly suffered a terrible debilitating illness, a disease of the spine from which she was sadly paralysed for the rest of her life. Now an invalid, Nelly became confined to her room in Padstow. She began collecting notebooks of impressions from her view out of her bedroom window. Then she wrote children's novels, which were published under the name Nellie Cornwall. Nelly developed a keen interest in Cornish folklore, especially tales of piskeys. In time, local people came to tell her folk tales, which she wrote in her notebooks then wrote them up under the name of Enys Tregarthen. She published three popular collections of North Cornwall's folk tales. The scholar Simon Young distinguished between what he called her 'collected' and 'concocted' tales and has identified the traditional tales in Enys's work. In chapters 11 and 12 are some of the tales she collected.

THE PISKEY'S REVENGE

There was once a turf-cutter who lived on the Cornish moors with his wife and their grandchild, Genefer. Granfer Nankivell spent his days out on the moor cutting turf and Granny spent hers baking. She baked a lot of sweet food as Granfer had a very sweet tooth. He was especially pleased when Granny made junket (a milky pudding like yogurt) and sugar biscuits.

One day, old Granfer Nankivell was out on the moor cutting turf as every day, but this day he cleared a bog. Pleased with his work, he set out home. Now, the piskeys were angry because they slept on the soft, green grasses of the peat bog and they wanted revenge on Granfer for cutting it all into turfs. The piskeys set out their piskey-lights ready to confuse Granfer, so that he would get lost in the bogs on his way home. Granfer Nankivell saw the piskey-lights but he wasn't led astray as the piskeys had hoped. Granfer was wise to the piskey ways and he had made sure to turn his pockets inside out to protect himself from being piskey led.

The piskeys were still angry to have lost their beds and they still wanted revenge. They decided to find a way to upset Granfer and took to watching him wherever he went. Often the piskeys liked to dance or to set out their piskey-lights, but they always had someone watching Granfer.

The piskeys noticed something particular; Granfer had a sweet tooth. It was the evening before Granfer's birthday and Granny wanted to make him some especially yummy sugar biscuits to eat. She and Genefer spent a long time making them just right. The junket and biscuits were left in the spence (pantry) on a stone table by an open window looking out over the moors. When Genefer looked in the morning every crumb had been eaten.

'Granny, Granfer's birthday treats have been eaten,' Genefer cried.

'I'm so disappointed to miss out on my birthday treat,' said Granfer. 'I think it's the piskeys.'

'I think it's Genefer is eating it all,' said Granny crossly.

'It's not me,' said Genefer. 'I'm as upset as Granfer.'

That night, Granny decided to make some more junket and a tray of sugar biscuits. When they were ready, she laid them out on the table in the spence. She looked out of the window across the moors but she couldn't see any piskeys. She bolted the window all the same. The piskeys waited for Granny to go to bed and crept into Granny's spence and ate everything. This would punish Granfer Nankivell for cutting turf from the piskeys' soft beds. When in the morning, Granny Nankivell found everything had been eaten, she called for Genefer.

'Genefer, have you eaten all my junket?' Granny asked.

'I think it was the cat,' said Granfer. 'Not our Genefer.'

'A cat might eat the junket but it would not easily have eaten a whole tray of biscuits. Really, Genefer,' scolded her Granny.

'Next time you make junket,' said Genefer trying not to cry, 'look through the keyhole to the spence, and it won't be me you see.'

The next day, Granny made her sweet foods again and put them in the spence for safekeeping. Instead of going to sleep, Granny got up and went to the spence. As the moon rose, she stood by the door and looked through the keyhole, just as Genefer had suggested. Piskeys were everywhere, spooning out junket and eating biscuits. They were passing biscuits out of the window to a line of piskeys streaming across the moor. Granny opened the door and shouted, 'I'll have you all in here doing my housework, washing Granfer's socks and scrubbing the floor. You should be ashamed for taking Granfer's biscuits!' Every little piskey disappeared and Genefer was never doubted again.

There are still Nankivells living on Bodmin Moor to this day, and there are still piskeys …

SKERRY WERRY

It had been raining on the moors all winter. A constant gloom rolled over the fading bracken. A lonely woman went about her chores, keeping her peat fire burning and tending to the house. It was a wonder she was so careful to keep things in order, for she had no husband and no children she could call her own. One night when the rain hit loudly against the windows and the wind roared down the chimney, there came a fast knocking at the door. The woman went to open it, puzzled for she never had visitors. It was very dark outside and the rain muscled in and stung her face. Bravely she peered out into the blackness. There on her well-brushed doormat, stood a child of the little people. It lifted its arms up, bold as can be.

'Skerry Werry needs a mummy,' it cried.

Now the woman had always longed for children. It would hardly hurt to pick up this poor abandoned child and take it in out of the cold, even if it were so clearly a piskey child. She bent down and carefully scooped up the tiny child onto the palm of her hand and took it inside.

'Skerry Werry needs a mummy. Will you be my mummy?' asked the child again.

The lonely woman couldn't help but feel herself fill with joy as she took the child to her fireside rocking chair and sat it on her lap. The lonely woman rocked Skerry Werry long into the night. As she rocked, Skerry Werry got heavier and heavier until the woman struggled to hold him on her lap. She tried to hold him around his middle and rock her chair, but his weight pushed them backwards against the wall, and the child cried out in his sleep. The lonely woman peered hard at the child, its soft brown hair and bronze skin lit with candlelight. His body squirmed in her lap. Feeling the weight of him, the lonely woman wondered if she was dreaming.

She tried to get up to lay the child down but Skerry Werry started to whine in a high-pitched voice, 'All I need is for you to hold me and be my mummy.' The woman wrapped the growing child in her skirts and began to slowly rock her chair. She did her best to mummy him but he seemed to get heavier and heavier until the woman winced in pain at the load of him. He reached up to hang his arms on her shoulders snuggling in and she thought she would soon burst beneath him. Having a heavy sleeping lump on her lap wasn't at all how she had imagined being a mother and the woman began to cry.

Unable to sleep herself, the woman stared out of the window into the darkness and all at once she thought she saw a light flicker and disappear. She heaved Skerry Werry onto the seat of the chair, at the same time edging herself out of it and tiptoed to the door.

The woman looked helplessly out onto the dark moor. The rain was relentless. A thick mist hung over the moor, then a ring of yellow formed in the blackness and grew brighter. Piskey lights swung across the moor in the direction of the house. All at once, at her doorstep was a piskey lady with long brown hair and big brown eyes.

'I have come for my little Skerry Werry,' she said simply.

'Mummy,' said Skerry Werry, and all of a sudden, he was small as she and he ran into his mummy's arms.

TALES FROM NORTH CORNWALL'S COAST

PADSTOW

'Ere we'm off to Summercourt Fair
Me mother said, "'ess",
Me father said, "No,"
An' dash me buttons if I dunt't go.'

The north coast of Cornwall is noticeably different to the south coast. Steep rocky cliffs rise above towering seas and wild Atlantic waves. The north coast is a surfer's paradise and surfers ride Cornish waves all year round. The sea breaks above long beaches decked with sand dunes and sweeping sands. The land is more open and flatter; there are less hills, and less woods. The trees in the hedges are stunted and flowering in pretty whites and pinks. In places, the eye can see right across the fields to the moors in the distance. The fishing port of Padstow is surrounded by breathtakingly beautiful bays. Remembering her experience of these bays, Enys Tregarthen collected and wrote many tales set along the coast near to her home town.

Constantine Bay illustrates the wild and divine nature of the beaches along Cornwall's north coast. The bay is just a couple of miles along the coast from Padstow. The approach to the beach is along a path through sand dunes. With the tide out on a day in May, the sumptuous tan-gold sand reaches out to a spread of rock pools and on into the sea. There is a sweeping semicircle of dunes behind the beach, decked with cliffs and headlands on either edge. Constantine church, featuring in Jan Brewer's tale, has been lost to the elements, like many a Cornish church or house built on the wind-ravished cliffs, and has crumbled away over the years.

A constant crashing of waves can be heard above the barking of dogs and the chatter of families on the beach, a reminder Constantine is nature's bay. Looking out to sea, behind the shadow of sea mists, are rocky islands. The rock pools are glassy mirrors, many coloured nets dipping in, making ripples on the surface.

How Jan Brewer was Piskey Laden

Jan Brewer was on his way home to his cottage on the cliffs at Constantine. The tide was out and the moon was up and before going home Jan went to forage in the rock pools strewn across the sands. The pools were pretty in the moonlight; weeds of purples and greens swirled in the water, covering shells and a flicker of movement. He took off his shoes and soft sand shaped between his toes. He took off his hat and the wind blew his hair across his eyes. He kept on his coat as it was chilly on the beach. Jan took such a time exploring in the rock pools of Constantine Bay, that the moon was high in a dark sky over the sea and night had come without him realising the passing of time.

Jan left the beach and climbed the dunes up onto the cliffs and rambled along to the ruined church. He loved the eerie glow of moonlight on stone and imagined the building candlelit, songs drifting out to sea, and he let his mind wander as he clambered about. He stopped to listen as he was certain he heard laughter; tinkling laughter surrounding him in a ring of sound. *It's probably just the sea birds*, Jan thought to himself, although come to think of it he couldn't see any. Jan blinked as lanterns appeared before his eyes, tiny swaying lanterns flickering all about him. Well Jan had wished for candlelight and song, and quickly he realised he was surrounded by a ring of piskeys dancing all about him. Jan knew all about the piskeys; they laugh and sing and dance in a ring. Before he knew it, Jan was dancing with them round and round across the common, his hair flapping and his bare feet tapping. Round and round whirled Jan Brewer and he couldn't have stopped if he tried.

Dizzy and mazed, Jan tried to think, and he knew only one thing – he was piskey laden. Jan reached deep into his coat and turned his pockets inside out. In an instant, every tiny piskey vanished as did their lanterns and their song. Jan sat for a while in the tufty grass. When he had stopped feeling dizzy and mazed, Jan Brewer picked himself up and found his way home.

The Small People's Fair

Near Constantine is a lane called Tresallyn. Many people have thought they could hear piskeys laughing when walking along this lane but very few have seen them.

Hender Bennett was walking along Tresallyn Lane on his way back from Towan village. The evening was ahum with insects, the sky was clear and the sea air was cool around Hender's ears. He almost missed a second hum of chattering voices and a clatter of exchanging coins, just audible beneath the distant crash of the waves. Hender stopped in the middle of the lane and peered closely all about him. Along the verge were a string of little stalls selling all manner of tiny wares; vegetables, cakes, clothes, seashell jewellery, posies of pink campion and cowslip; anything you would expect to see at a Cornish village fair. Except this was no ordinary village fair; this dainty fair was full of piskeys. Hender watched the comings and goings of the piskeys' fair for a long time. He loved the excitement on their faces as they made deals, bought and sold. He watched as they ate and drank, danced and sang.

All at once they began to dance around and around in many rings all down the lane. Hender thought he would never find his way home without catching them beneath his great big boots. He crouched down so as to take a better look at the stall with pretty posies of wild flowers.

'I think I will take one of these for my wife,' Hender said gaily, taking out a coin and throwing it to the ground. The piskey stallholder shouted to his companions, speaking wildly, accusing Hender of piskey sight, and in an instant the piskeys and their fair vanished from Tresallyn Lane. In its place, shadows grew along the verges and clouds rolled in from the sea. Jan could just make out the absence of his coin and in its place lay a posy of cowslips. He carefully picked it up to take home and lay on the pillow of his wife.

MOTHER IVEY

Between Constantine and Padstow are Mother Ivey's Bay, Harlyn Bay and Hawker's Cove. This is the story of Mother Ivey.

Mother Ivey was a white witch living at Trevose Head, the other side of the headland to Harlyn Bay. A vocal member of the community, Ivey tried to sort out any trials or misunderstandings as best she could. She used her charms and spells for righting harm and wrongs, and was very seldom angry. One man who lived in Harlyn tried Mother Ivey's kindness. Bad idea to try a witch, even a white one.

In those days Harlyn's wealth was in silver; the silver of pilchards caught and salted and sent to Italy for Catholic folk to eat on fish Fridays and in Lent. The silver lined the cellars of the fish merchant, but when the fish went to Italy, it didn't fill the bellies of the Cornish fishermen's families.

A fish merchant lived at a house called The Fish Cellars, still at Harlyn Bay today, and he had a very successful business selling pilchards. His house had a motto carved into the granite lintel over the door. It said, 'Profit Smells Sweet'. In contrast to the success and profit made at the fish cellars, the villagers were starving.

One week, a ship carrying a large cargo of pilchards was returned from Italy unsold. Every villager came to see the ship in. They were hopeful their bellies would soon be filled. The fish merchant took the fish off the ship and up the hill to his farm. Mother Ivey pleaded with him to allow the villagers to eat the fish as it was still good enough to eat, even though it could not be sold.

Instead, the fish were ploughed into a field as fertiliser. Mother Ivey was very angry; the people she spent her years helping were in desperate need of the food that had just been denied them. She went to the Fish Cellars and cursed the merchant's field.

'Break the soil. Death will follow.'

And it did. The next year, the merchant ploughed the field and planted corn. A few weeks later his eldest son was out riding his horse, when he fell off and was killed.

Profit smelled sour. No one has taken a spade or a plough to the field since, for fear of what may happen. The field lies fallow to this day.

But Mother Ivey's kindness lives on as well as her curse; kindness in the hearts of the lifeboat men stationed at Mother Ivey's bay, willing to risk their lives to save their fellow men from the silvery sea.

Reefy, Reefy Rum

The best way to approach the fishing port of Padstow is by bicycle. The Camel Trail runs alongside the Camel Estuary. Across the river are fields, hedges, sheep and the edges of moorland. The trail enters Padstow alongside the harbour. The harbour is extensive with lots of trawlers, smaller fishing boats and sailing boats with masts straining into the sky. Alongside the quay is a constant motion of visitors walking by or sitting along the wall, their feet dangling over the edge, the water still, deep, bottle green. Heading out to sea, the river is crossed by the Doom Bar, a bar of golden sand placed there by the mermaid of Padstow in revenge at Tristan Bird for foolishly shooting her in a pool at Hawker's Cove.

Padstow residents remember being piskey laden; they went into the fields and came out feeling disorientated. To the people of Padstow, the River Camel was thought to heal and provide everything; fish would be traded for vegetables and people didn't bother with doctors, they just washed cuts in the river. Richer families were very aware of poorer families and all lived together around the harbour. There was

*lots of handing down of possessions and clothes so the poor didn't go
without. Richer children would be asked to pick out toys to be given
away to poorer children. In days gone by the community of Padstow
looked after everyone.*

*Nellie Sloggett was born in Duke Street, where she lived as a child.
She then moved to Cross Street, where she lived in her 20s. From
the age of 30 to 50 she lived with her uncle, Charles Rawle. Charles
Rawle's family lived in Marine Villa, behind the Institute village
hall, opposite the harbour. Her uncle was a shipbuilder and had
worked his way up to be an important member of Padstow society.
He provided for his invalid niece and her mother for many years; an
example of Padstow community spirit. If you stand on the quay and
look out, you can see St Minver and Sand Hills. In Marine Villa she
wrote her collections of Cornish folk tales,* The Piskey Purse *and* The
Legends of North Cornwall.

*Stone statues have captured the imaginations of the children of
Padstow for generations. For hundreds of years, high up on the front
of the grand house in the market square, sat two little horsemen. One
night, the two stone horsemen came alive and chased a little boy all
around the streets of Padstow and back to the market square. Here's
another stone tale.*

Alice Rawle loved to walk about the streets of Padstow. She played
by the quay, watching the boats, she played on the streets with her
friends, she ran errands for her mother and, best of all, she liked to
skip up the lane leading to the churchyard. Once inside the gate,
Alice went straight to the south wall. Up on three stone buttresses sat
three stone figures; a stone lion, a stone unicorn and a stone knight
with a shield. She sat among the daisies and wondered how it would
be if the three stone figures came to life. Would she be terribly frightened and run for her life or would she stand firm and fight them off?

One day Alice was feeling raw. Her mother had told her off and
Alice was sitting in the churchyard sulking. She stood up to get
a closer look at the figures sitting high above her and their stony
eyes stared straight ahead. They were ignoring Alice. She shouted
up at them.

'Reefy, reefy, rum,
without teeth or tongue;
if you'll have me,
now I am come.'

She waited a few moments, her eyes never leaving the statues but nothing happened. The lion, the unicorn and the knight never even blinked.

The next time Alice got a chance, she went to the churchyard and stood looking up at the lion. Alice would like to ride a lion, she would like to show him off to her friends. Alice would lead the lion by a soft rope and bury her arms in his mane. If she was feeling especially kind, she would allow her friends to stroke him but only she would ride him through the town and down onto the sands. There the lion would run faster than wind, stronger than the tide. Alice called up to the lion,

'Reefy, reefy, rum,
without teeth or tongue;
if you'll have me,
now I am come.'

The lion didn't move; he was true to his rigid stone. Alice went sadly home.

The next time Alice and her mother had quarrelled, she ran through the streets of Padstow and up to the churchyard. She looked up hopefully at the little knight. He appeared young and brave and also strong. His shield was nearly as big as he was; he had to have strength to carry it. Alice wondered what he had done with his sword – perhaps it was tied to his back. Alice imagined her friends' envy as she walked through town with a knight. She would hide behind his great shield and jump out to surprise them. Alice called up to the knight,

'Reefy, reefy, rum,
without teeth or tongue;
if you'll have me,
now I am come.'

For a moment nothing stirred and then, all at once, the three statues came to life and jumped off the church wall. Alice hesitated, then she began to run. The lion, the knight and the unicorn ran after her. Looking over her shoulder Alice could see the lion's fierce eyes and lean body. Perhaps he would catch her in one leap. The knight didn't look friendly at all; he certainly wasn't shouting out a truce or offering to protect her. The unicorn pranced sideways, shaking her mane and snorting to the winds. Her four hooves kicked up stones, her legs were strong, her eyes mean. What had Alice unleashed by taunting the statues on the church wall? Would she ever see her mother again? The open gate was only a few steps away and Alice threw herself through it. As she fell, she kicked the gate closed with her foot, expecting the lion and the unicorn to leap over it. She waited moments but there was silence. They had stopped at the gate and, turning around, they walked solemnly back to their positions on the church wall. Although Alice occasionally visited them throughout her life, she never dared to repeat the rhyme. The lion, the knight and the unicorn have never yet moved again.

WHY JAN PENDOGGIT CHANGED HIS MIND

Jan Pendoggit was a young farmer who lived with his mother on a farm near Padstow. It was September and the day of the annual Summercourt Fair, the oldest fair in Cornwall. He was to walk 12 miles by road from Padstow to Summercourt. Jan had live-stock to sell and he would be gone most of the day.

'You make sure you avoid the piskey rings on your way home mind,' said his mother.

'Piskey rings? Don't you worry, Mother. I've never come across piskeys in the fields. I don't think I will suddenly see them today.'

'You be sure to turn your pockets or your jacket inside out, soon as they catch you.'

'Don't you go worrying, Mother. I will be fine.'

The fair was crowded and the trade was good. All the animals Jan had brought with him sold. Jan left early evening and set off back along the road to Padstow. Being late September, the

evenings were losing their light and it was soon dusky black, the
hedgerows dark thickets, the track visible just a step ahead. Jan's
feet hurt and he ached with tiredness but he was nearly home and
he had a few meadow fields to cross on his way up to his farm.

As he crossed the second field with his farm almost in sight, Jan
had an uneasy feeling he was no longer alone. He listened for the
bark of a fox, the scuttle of a badger along the edges of the hedge,
perhaps the swoop and hoot of an owl or a gull overhead. The
meadow was strangely void of fauna, lost was the summer buzz
of insects in the grasses; now something else lingered in the fields
and Jan couldn't quite put his finger on what it was.

First, he heard a laugh, then he saw a light and in moments the whole field was lit with rings of piskey lanterns swinging to the motion of a fast piskey dance. And Jan couldn't find his way through them: he tried to shuffle forwards, he tried running and then sitting down in the long grass but even that didn't shelter him. Enveloping his every sense, from all directions, was the motion of the piskey dance. Jan was soon dancing round and round. He could see the little people now; men and women in little green and red outfits having the time of their lives, dancing in the meadow. But Jan wasn't enjoying the dance; he was hungry and tired and wished himself home. As the dance got faster and faster and the piskey laughter louder and louder, Jan felt himself become dizzy and confused with no idea how to get himself free.

Just as Jan was beginning to think he would be spending the rest of his days in a piskey ring, he remembered his mother's advice. He took off his jacket and turned it inside out. The piskey lights went out and the music and laughter disappeared, the piskeys with it. Jan was alone in the meadow once more. He hastened to the gap in the hedge he could usually have found with his eyes closed and was up the path and inside the farmhouse, quick as his legs would carry him.

'You warned me Mother about the piskey rings and I didn't believe you,' he cried to his mother who sat waiting for him in her rocking chair by the fire. 'Now I, Jan Pendoggit, have changed my mind.'

13

TINTAGEL AND
BOSCASTLE

'Tis an ill wind blows no good to Cornwall.'

*Breathing beneath the clamour of Arthurian visitors, an air of majesty
wreaths Tintagel. This ruined castle on the cliffs of North Cornwall is
the seat of ancient kings. Remembered only by the swirling mists and
lashing winds, a baby was born at Tintagel Castle; a baby who grew
up to be King Arthur himself. King Arthur's story and his connections
to Tintagel were written down in the twelfth century by Geoffrey of
Monmouth and have been retold ever since. The castle was built in
the thirteenth century by the first Earl of Cornwall, but there have
been settlements at Tintagel since Roman times, when it was an
important link in trading with the Mediterranean. The village itself
has amongst many places of interest to tourists; a visitors' centre, a
medieval hall called the Old Post Office, an Arthurian centre, gal-
leries, gift shops and tearooms. Along the bottom of a valley between
cliffs, a path takes a steady stream of visitors down to the remains of
Tintagel Castle, which is now under English Heritage stewardship.*

*A strong wind blows in from the sea, black rooks circle the fields,
a gold light rests on the cliffs. Next to the castle lays the ruins of the
chapel. Tintagel Castle's Chapel once held a bell; the Chapel Bell
rang for the adventurous lady Serena, to call her home to the castle.
Near Tintagel is St Nectan's Glen and Kieve. To get to St Nectan's
Kieve, there is an enchanting walk through a woodland valley with*

the River Trevillet flowing alongside. Climbing through the woods, the sound of the 60ft waterfall grows. Pure white tumbling water falls against black slate, edged with bright green mosses. Standing beneath and looking up, the waterfall is mesmerising, a truly magical beauty in nature.

St Nectan's Kieve and the Lonely Sisters

At Trevillet in the parish of Tintagel, on a pile of rocks, deep in the woods, lay the chapel of St Nectan. The chapel was concealed with trees from passers-by but visible to those out at sea. In the tower of his chapel, St Nectan hung a silver bell, which he would ring to warn sailors of a coming storm. Sailors came to know the ringing of the bell and took the sound as a sign St Nectan was praying for them. They would be safe from harm on the stormy seas.

At that time there was a struggle within the Church. St Nectan was very wary of incomers and their threat to his Celtic faith. He prophesied this faith would be almost lost save for a tiny spark. He told the people of Tintagel he was going to hide his bell within the rocks of the Kieve. The bell was to be left there until a time when true faith was restored to Cornwall. 'My bell will only ring for a true believer!' he said. Nectan rang his bell three times and dropped it into the waters of the Kieve where it disappeared, never yet to be found.

Sometime after this, St Nectan died. As if out of nowhere, two strange sisters came and buried St Nectan, his treasure and possessions from the chapel in a large chest. They diverted the course of the river and dug a hole big enough for the chest. They buried the chest and in an instant, the river flowed back over the buried saint.

The sisters lived at the chapel and were self-sufficient, never troubling the villagers for anything. Curious, the villagers of Trevillet tried to find out who the ladies were but the two never said a word. One sister died and the villagers watched helpless as one cried over the other. They helped the living sister to remove the body and left her to grieve. No one heard any more of her, until a child went to peer in the window and there found the second woman motionless, quite dead. The people buried the woman under a large slab of rock in the river.

Many years later, a group of miners came to St Nectan's Kieve. They diverted the river to work on the rock. They bored holes in the rock but it didn't budge. Instead, a voice was heard amongst the ringing of tools.

'The child is not yet born who will this treasure recover.'

The work was stopped and the river restored to its natural course. And if you listen carefully at St Nectan's Kieve, amongst the birdsong, lapping river and roaring waterfall, you may be the one with the purest of faith, Celtic faith, who will once again hear the ringing of St Nectan's bell.

THE WIND WITCHES

Just along the coast from Tintagel is Boscastle, a harbour village decked in trees. Woodland rises on either side of a steep valley. All feels calm but Boscastle is on the cusp of the sea. The harbour walls are built high, shielding. There are lots of fishing boats and a huge pile of lobster pots. The cliffs begin with jutting slate and are topped with grasses rolling in the wind. Climbing up from the harbour onto the cliffs, the calm wind blowing along the harbour is replaced with a battering wind from the sea. Boscastle's tale twists these very winds.

Jowen held a piece of rope firmly, a rope with three knots, that he took with him on every voyage. Sometimes he would untie one knot and a gentle breeze blew through his dark hair. Once he had untied the second knot and a fair wind jostled his boat. Never had he untied the third knot as legend had it the witches of Boscastle would conjure a storm.

Gwen held the answer to the wind between her hands. The rope was knotted three times. The wind witches' ropes they called them; all the sailors had one with them as they sailed from Boscastle off toward the horizon. Gwen watched Jowen and his boat leave the harbour. She untied the first knot and called a gentle breeze to blow him out to sea. She untied a second knot and called a fair wind to rock him back and forth between rising waves. She untied the third knot and a strange sound filled the harbour and raged out to sea. The sound of a storm gathering, the sound of a storm breaking.

FORRABURY BELLS

Boscastle is within two parishes, Minster and Forrabury. The harbour part of Boscastle is in the parish of Forrabury and Forrabury Church is Boscastle's church. Between Forrabury Church and Willapark Cliffs are the Forrabury Strips, a series of forty-two strips of field farmed in plots 'stitch meal', a method of crop rotation used from Celtic times to the present day. Looked after by the National Trust, Forrabury Strips are very special as only three places in Britain use the strip method today. Willapark Cliffs edge Boscastle; they also look out over the sea at Western Blackapit. Throughout the ages the bay of Western Blackapit has been a black spot for shipwrecks.

Forrabury, a small village west of Boscastle, was and still is a village without bells. The people of Forrabury wanted beautiful bells, ones to rival the regal vesper bells at Tintagel. Tintagel's bells had rung for the birth and death of King Arthur. Forrabury's bells would run away with the wind, ringing across the sea, marking every occasion. There was nowhere that made bells in Forrabury; the Forrabury Bells were cast far away and would be delivered by ship. The arrival of the bells was a big occasion: stalls were laid out, musicians played and the village girls danced. The hour the ship arrived in the bay at Western Blackapit, there was a dream of a sea and a fair wind drifted waiting for the tide to bring her to shore.

Tintagel's vesper bell rang out and the thin, tense pilot of the ship crossed himself praying, thanking the Lord for the voyage and asking for a safe landing. The captain of the ship, who was a big, rugged man with a great, beefy beard, laughed at the pilot praying to the Lord.

'Don't you go thanking 'ee. It was I steered this ship so swiftly and I alone.'

'God forgive you,' said the pilot, looking uneasily about him.

The people of Forrabury walked along the Forrabury Stitches to Willapark Cliffs. They gathered looking out at the ship in the bay at Western Blackapit and waited for their bells to be delivered. They felt the rub of the fair wind on their bare arms strengthen to a stinging swipe and knew the sea was about to change her mood. A communal gasp rose above the wind as the onlookers saw an enormous wave rise above the ship enveloping it and claiming the bells to be rung in the arms of the sea. As the ship sank, the Forrabury Bells were heard ringing out the deaths of the many sailors aboard. Of a ship full of men only the thin pilot survived.

To this day, when a storm is coming to ravage the north coast of Cornwall, the Forrabury Bells can be heard ringing a warning from deep within the sea.

THE PISKEY WHO RODE IN A POCKET

'Piskeys are full of Mischief.'

South of Boscastle, along the Valency Valley, is Minster Wood. The river runs through the trees and out into the harbour. Walking through Minster Wood, there are lots of butterflies fluttering amongst a soft foliage of ferns, logs and reeds: a sweet smell of wood mulch and blackberries and the sound of the water in the river and of bees passing by. Nature is busy here, just the place for piskeys.

Near Boscastle is a place called Minster Woods and in the fields and moors around these woods, live lots and lots of piskeys. The piskeys are very busy beings, getting people into bother and causing mischief. A lot has been told here about piskeys. They especially love to steal horses, junket and biscuits. Into the manes and tails of stolen horses, they plait stirrups and panniers. The horses gallop away with three or four piskeys hanging from their tails and three or four piskeys riding their manes, all the piskeys shrieking with glee. At night, the piskeys light lanterns near the bogs to lead poor, unsuspecting walkers into the marshy water.

These tasks the piskeys did every day until one piskey thought he would like a different adventure. The piskey wore a long red riding coat, green hat and green trousers. He had sparkly brown eyes and long whiskers. Happy with his plan, the piskey danced across the moors laughing.

'What fun I'm going to have,' he giggled.

Dancing off the moors, he came to Minster Woods and a road leading to Lesnewth. The piskey climbed onto a rock and waited. He watched lots of people walking past on their way to do their shopping in Boscastle. The piskey saw everybody but not one of them saw the piskey. Evening came and the piskey sat on his stone, watching the people go by, their bags full of shopping. At last, along came an elderly woman; she was the one he had been waiting for. The piskey leaped off his stone, caught hold of her dress and swung himself up into her pocket.

Now the woman had been quite sure where she was going until the moment the piskey landed in her pocket, when she became instantly confused and unsure of her surroundings.

'I came through Boscastle, up through Minster woods … I am unable to find my way all of a sudden. I must get back before darkness.'

The woman took a wrong path through the woods, walking away from Lesnewth. 'I must be mazed,' she said to herself, more and more confused as to her whereabouts. As she walked, she huffed and puffed and pulled on her pocket.

The little piskey laughed. 'This is the ride of my life!'

Darkness fell; trees cast giant shadows, boughs creaked, owls hooted and bats squeaked. The piskey enjoyed every moment of his ride. The lady became more and more lost until she sat herself down on a tree trunk.

'Of course, how silly of me not to remember, I must turn my pockets inside out. I must have a piskey somewhere about me. I must be piskey laden.'

She turned her pockets inside out, and out fell the little man with the green hat, red riding britches and boots and rolled along the path. The elderly lady cried out in surprise as she saw him. She tried to work out which path to take and almost cried in frustration. All about her she heard piskey laughter. A little face peered round a tree trunk and she thought she might just as well follow him. As day broke, the piskey ran over a little bridge separating Minster and St Juliet's parishes. With a lovely day stretching out before her, the elderly lady went on her way home to Lesnewth.

MORWENSTOW
AND BUDE

'He was brought to us on the salt water
He was carried away by the wind.'

Morwenstow is the most northerly parish of Cornwall, with a church, farm and rectory cloaked in trees. The church at Morwenstow is on the cliff path set back a few fields away from the cliffs, its spire looking out to sea. In 1834 a new vicar came to Morwenstow Church, Parson Robert Hawker; the first parson Morwenstow had seen for over a hundred years. Smugglers and wreckers were rampant in the area. Wrecking was part of the smuggling trade; goods washed ashore were common property but every man on board had to have perished before it was legal to take from the ship. Many a ship was deliberately wrecked for its cargo off the north Cornish coast. Parson Hawker felt it was his duty to rescue sailors and give those who had died a church burial. A collector of tales and a writer of ballads, Parson Hawker wrote the Cornish anthem, 'Trelawney'. He built a hut out of driftwood on the cliffs in which he wrote his poems. Hawker's Hut is preserved today and is the smallest property owned by the National Trust. An eccentric man, Parson Hawker dressed in colourful clothes and liked to sit on rocks on the beach dressed as a mermaid as a joke. He had several animals as part of his congregation.

Nowadays, the thirteenth-century Rectory Farm Tea Rooms is adjacent to the church. Along a good sturdy cliff path, a strong sea wind batters the ears. Farmland stretches to the edge of the cliffs, a herd of cows sit chewing and sleeping by the path. The cliff fields are scattered with gold flowers and molehills. Ships sail past in clear view on a blue grey sea. The huge dark cliffs are jagged and formidable. Below, the sea is not always kind. The wild, exuberant and ruthless Atlantic has sunk many ships along the coast at Morwenstow. A smuggler and wrecker living on a Morwenstow farm wouldn't have had to leave the farmland to stand on the cliffs and signal to passing friends aboard ships or lure sailors to their doom on the ragged rocks below. A farmer's daughter wouldn't have had to leave her farm to stand on those same cliffs and watch her smuggler husband sail away.

CRUEL COPPINGER

One night a hurricane ravished the north coast. Just off the cliffs near Morwenstow a ship was wrecking on the rocks. Its sails were shredded and the rudder was gone. The whole ship swayed violently in the huge waves and was not going to stay afloat for very much longer. A crowd of terrified sailors gathered on deck; they knew their fate. One man held the wheel and shouted to the other men, clearly in charge. He lifted his fists and shook them at the winds. One moment he was in command of a sinking ship, the next he threw himself into the sea and rolled with the waves. The man was strong – he fought the battle of his life, rippling shoulders forcing a way against the sea and towards the shore. So fierce was the sailor, he overcame the wrath of the ocean and stood tall on the beach. The sands were crowded with wreckers and people watching the spectacle of the ship floundering at the mercy of the hurricane.

The sailor strode toward the crowd and ripped the coat off an elderly woman and then wrapped it over his naked torso. Next, he pushed his way to where a young woman sat watching from the safety of her saddle. He grabbed the reins from the hapless Dinah Hamlyn and leaped up behind her, spurring the horse into a gallop with his knees. The horse took its riders home and the sailor was warmed at the fireplace of farmer Hamlyn. The shipwrecked sailor made himself at home, telling the family he was from a wealthy Danish family and had spurned a titled lady to run away to sea. Dinah was instantly charmed, falling in love with the stranger and in days he proposed marriage. However, their wedding was postponed by the sudden death of the farmer. Farmer Hamlyn was not yet cold in his grave before the stranger moved to take charge of the household. He and Dinah were soon married.

This is when the mood at the farm changed. The strong, dashing stranger revealed himself to be Cruel Coppinger, captain of a gang of wreckers, smugglers, poachers and reprobates spanning the north coast. He sailed a large schooner called *The Black Prince* up and down the coast, menacing all who came across it. There were no revenue officers or law enforcers at that time and the local clergy were scared into submission. Cruel Coppinger did exactly what he liked, masterminding a reign of fear. Once an excise man challenged Coppinger, who chopped off the excise man's head with a sword. In doing so, Cruel Coppinger reinforced his reign of terror with this terrible act against authority. Anyone who challenged Coppinger was kidnapped and made to crew *The Black Prince*. Their families paid a fortune to get their loved ones home from the ship and for Coppinger the gold came rolling in.

Coppinger became so rich he bought another farm, heaping gold, pistols, guineas and ducats on the desk of a bewildered lawyer, who agreed to accept the sum in weight. He sailed up and down the coast in the schooner and hoarded all his loot in a cave. On the headland at Steeple Brink, the main tracks and bridleways across the fields became known as Coppinger's Tracks. These were impassable at night. He rode his tracks on a wild mare, strong and fast enough to make many quick escapes.

One of the clergymen decided it was time to speak out against the wrecker. One day, when this clergyman was riding home on his sedentary cob horse, Coppinger appeared on his mare. The mare reared up as he hurled a whip across the hapless clergyman's shoulders. The poor man knew he could not escape; the mare was known to be the fastest horse in all Cornwall. There was nothing for it; he would have to ride his cob home at a sensible pace, which he did with Cruel Coppinger just behind him, whipping him all the way. When they reached the clergyman's home, Coppinger shouted, 'I have paid my tithe,' and rode away.

One night at the farmhouse, Coppinger had been feasting. He was about to go out when he spotted a travelling tailor called Tom. Cruel Coppinger dragged the poor man into the yard, hoisted him onto the back of his mare and jumped on behind. The two men rode together, the mare becoming increasingly wild as they rode through the night. The tailor kept trying to launch himself off the mare and Coppinger fastened his belt to the tailor's, holding them together. Kicking the mare on into a punishing gallop, Cruel Coppinger shouted, 'I once told the devil I would find him a tailor and in you I have the devil's gift.'

They rode for miles, the mare never letting up on her speed. Suddenly the belt gave way and the tailor fell off into the bushes, where he was found quivering and muttering in the morning.

Coppinger and Dinah had a son who, from a young age, became as much a scoundrel as his father. In time, Cruel Coppinger's luck ran out and a king's cutter watched the coast from the sea. The king's cutter was ruthless in stopping all the smuggler's activities and Coppinger's business success was quickly finished. When he had spent his last gold piece, he went to the cliffs at Gull Rock and fired his gun to alert a passing ship. He was in luck and they sent a boat out to fetch him. Dinah and her son watched from the shore, never to see Cruel Coppinger again.

THE FIRST MOLE OF CORNWALL

Alice was a beautiful girl but proud and vain. She was the only daughter of her widowed mother and they lived together in Coombe, near Morwenstow. One day they had been invited to a grand banquet at Stow, home of Sir Beville Grenville, the king's general, and his very, very tall bodyguard, Anthony Payne. Now Alice really liked their host and she had dressed up in her best

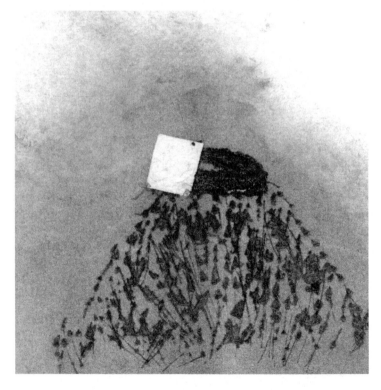

velvet dress and cloak. She hung lots of jewellery round her neck and from her ears, and she put a big diamond ring on her finger. Her mother said, 'All evening I will be praying he likes you as much as you do him.'

And Alice said, 'I see in the mirror, I look so lovely I will not need your prayer.'

All of a sudden, Alice cried out and she fell to the ground and disappeared forever.

The next day, the Coombe gardener discovered a small, unknown hillock with a sparkling ring on the top. The ring was the one Alice had worn but it had a new inscription on it,

'The earth must hide

Both eyes with pride.'

As he said the words, there was a small cry at his feet and a creature, clothed in velvet, groped around in darkness. She was the first mole of Cornwall.

THOMASINE BONAVENTURE

At the entrance to the beach at Bude, almost every eager passer-by is wearing a wetsuit and carrying a surfboard. Bude has a wide sandy bay with a sea water swimming pool. There is a canal where pedal and rowing boats can be hired. An audience sits on the green listening to an afternoon of jazz as part of Bude's annual Jazz Festival. Important to Bude's history is Sir Goldsworthy Gurney, born in 1793. A scientist, surgeon, architect, builder and inventor, he grew up in Cornwall but later moved to London. There he lectured in chemistry and invented a steam-powered vehicle. On his return to Cornwall, Gurney leased land overlooking Summerleaze Beach at Bude. He built The Castle on the sand hills. To light the Castle, he created the 'Bude Light' by forcing oxygen into an oil flame. The Castle still stands and has been extended. It is a good visit with a museum where exhibitions also take place. Bude town has a cheerful atmosphere focused on the sea, with a lot to be proud of. Along the cliffs from Bude is Widemouth Bay. The sun lights the sea, galloping waves shake pearly manes. A green haze lays on the cliffs.

*Week St Mary is a very friendly village on the way from Bude to
Launceston, surrounded by farmland. The village has a strong community spirit. The road centres around a memorial cross, where
there is a post office and general stores. The church and village green
are central to Week St Mary with many ancient stone houses and a
few thatched cottages surrounding them. Week St Mary's own Dick
Whittington is Thomasine Bonaventure.*

Thomasine Bonaventure worked on a farm with her father. She
fed and tended the sheep, collecting wood for the fire, scything
and pulling up weeds in the fields. Thomasine liked shearing time
best and as she folded up the fleece, the lanolin felt good, cooling
her poor, rough, chapped hands. Wool was big business in those
days and the Cornish sheep fleeces attracted merchants from all
over the country, although little money went to a poor family like
Thomasine's. They often went without and were cold in winter due
to lack of fuel for the fire. Sometimes her feet hurt and she became
tired when walking miles on the stony track to Launceston. She had
to walk the distance with her father on a regular basis while taking
sheep to market. Often Thomasine got wet feet wading through
the ford at Green-a-moor on the way to the farm. How she wished
there was a bridge, but the farmer was too mean to build one.

One day, when the young shepherdess was out looking after
her sheep, a merchant came by. He was lost on the moors travelling from London to Cornwall and he wanted to ask Thomasine
for directions. It was getting dark and there was little chance
he would find his way even with directions. She invited him to
supper and to stay with her family in their modest cottage. The
merchant liked Thomasine so much, he asked her parents if he
could enlist her services. They reluctantly agreed and the merchant took her with him to be a servant to his wife in London.

In London, Thomasine was beautifully polite and well-
mannered and much liked by both the merchant and his wife.
However, the merchant's wife was very unwell and on her
deathbed, she suggested to her husband that he marry young
Thomasine. The merchant attempted to gain Thomasine's love

and asked her to marry him. Soon after their marriage, the merchant also died and Thomasine inherited his money. With her inheritance she paid for a bridge to be built at Green-a-moor; her family would never again need to get their feet wet in the ford.

Bonaventure is a name meaning good fortune and after a time, Thomasine married again, a man with even more money. Having enjoyed the change of scene in London and all the new people and experiences of city life, she met and married Henry Gall, a wealthy merchant adventurer. Thomasine married Henry not for his money but for his sense of adventure. Henry was a fun and charming man. He liked to have Thomasine at his side and involve her in his adventures. He had many ships and they sailed together down the English Channel. As a wedding gift, Thomasine asked Henry if he might buy land for the poor of Week St Mary. They bought a communal wood where families such a Thomasine's might find wood for their fires in winter. Sadly, Henry also died, leaving Thomasine all his money, property and possessions and she became a very wealthy woman.

Thomasine was extremely sad at Henry's death as she had loved him and the life of a wife to a merchant adventurer where she had learned a lot. She was now a wealthy widow, living alone in the city of London with the nuisance of a large number of suitors who fancied themselves as the husband of a woman of great wealth.

Climbing even higher up into London society, Thomasine married Sir John Percival, a banker who, soon after their marriage, became the Lord Mayor of London. Thomasine Bonaventure, the Cornish farm maid, was now Lady Mayoress of the City of London. Never having forgotten the memories of struggling along the inadequate paths with her father, she used her wealth to build a proper paved road across the moor from Launceston to the sea, via Green-a-moor, where only rough paths had lain before. Thomasine also rebuilt the tower of St Stephen-by-Launceston.

When Sir John died, Thomasine returned to Green-a-moor as Lady Thomasine Percival, an enormously wealthy and well-connected woman. Being kind as well as wealthy, Lady Thomasine opened Week St Mary Grammar School. The special thing about

Thomasine's school was it was free to local children. She also helped all the local charities and is remembered for amassing such a fortune by accident and using it for good in her home village in Cornwall.

Cornwall is a beautiful, magical land but life was and often still is harsh and terribly poor. Amongst a life of hardship and frequent tragedy, the Cornish people have often found themselves in need of good luck. Real-life legends like that of the life of Thomasine Bonaventure are retold and fondly remembered as inspiring and hopeful. Cornish folk tales are entwined with the natural world and the outdoor nature of Cornish lives and work. Nature spirits exist betwixt and between human endeavour. From farmers to mothers, the people live reliant on nature. Piskeys in these tales have been seen to be helping the farmer, the elderly woman, the lonely child. Making their hard lives a little easier, a little more bearable and haven't we all wished for a little hint of kindness when life is unforgiving?

Little folk inhabit the edges between humans and nature. We have heard how the piskeys dance in rings at twilight, on the edge of the cliffs below the moon, in the hedgerows and marshlands and ride their horses into villages, far over open moorland and play with human children in the bright light of day. We have heard tales of the wicked being chased down the devil's dandy hole. Of saints overcoming giants, of witches cursing and healing and forgiving, of a mermaid who punished a town and of the ghost of a girl who saved the sailors of another. Within all these tales of Cornwall we glean a little of her magnificent land and people.

THE ILLUSTRATORS

Introduction
White Hare of Looe, Nicky Harwood, Liskeard

Chapter 1
The Fisherman and the Piskeys, CLASS 1, Looe
Colman Grey, CLASS 1, Looe
The Midwife's Tale, Peter Carew, Dobwalls

Chapter 2
The Spectral Coach, Henry Blencowe, Launceston
The White Hare of Looe, Alexander Ronaldson, Liskeard
The Cock-crow Stone, Jo Landrigan, Liskeard
Joseph of Arimathea visits Looe, Summer Spence, Looe
Amram and Jochabed, Charlie Garner and Ashton Moore, Looe

Chapter 3
The Seaton Mermaid, Amelia Franklin, Looe
A Voyage with the Piskeys, Milly Ritchie, Launceston
Finnygook, Archie Borlase, Looe

Chapter 4
Lady Mount Edgcumbe's Ring, Cindy Hill, Launceston
Patten Peg, Gen Oozergeer, Egloskerry
The Witch and the Toad, Ruby Berryman, Egloskerry
Blackberry Round, Yvette Hoskin, Liskeard
Dando and his Dogs, Nixie Dismore, Liskeard

King of the Cormorants, Tristan Ronaldson, Liskeard
A Ghostly Feast at Bethany, collage, Lauceston

Chapter 5
Saint Keyne, Maddie Hidson, Looe
Saint Cuby, Luke Jackson and Jack Priest, Looe
Saint Nona, Muki Fox, Bodmin

Chapter 6
The Legend of the Cheesewring, Elowen and Evie Doney, Liskeard
The Angel and the Cockerel, Elowen and Evie Doney, Liskeard
The Rillaton Cup, Donna Hillman, Launceston
The Old Storm Woman, Holly Clines, Egloskerry
Piskey Led, Grace Dunn, Dobwalls
Figgy Hobbin, Sue Field, Artist

Chapter 7
The Piskeys and the Housework, Charlie Bowden, Looe
King Alfred and King Dungarth, Sue Field, artist
The Phantom Beast, Sophie Fordham, artist
The Piskey who Lost his Laugh, Tarryn Mollard, Dobwalls

Chapter 8
The Challenge, John Roberts. PuppetCraft
Caradoc Gets the Girl, John Roberts, PuppetCraft
Caradoc Briefbras, John Roberts, PuppetCraft
The Mantle, John Roberts, PuppetCraft

Chapter 9
The Ghost of Dockacre, Andi Snook, Launceston
Digory Piper, Silas Sutton, Dobwalls
Betsy Laundry, Eloise Frances, Egloskerry

Chapter 10
The Piskey Warriors, Albert Blencoe, Launceston
Tristan and Isolde, Mark Gregory, artist

Chapter 11

Piskeys on the Mare's Neck, Riley Pownall, Dobwalls

Boy Who Played with the Piskeys, Elisha Williams, Bodmin

The Piskey's Revenge, Stephen Lambert, artist

Skerry Werry, Acha Fox, Bodmin

Chapter 12

How Jan Brewer was Piskey Laden, Finlay Dunn, Dobwalls

The Small People's Fair, George Southward, Bodmin

Mother Ivey, Alex Goodman, artist

Jan Pendoggit Changed his Mind, Mark Gregory

Chapter 13

St Nectan's Kieve, Sophie Hillman, Launceston

The Wind Witches, Evie Gillbard, Egloskerry'

Forabury Bells, Kerry Hillman, Launceston'

The Piskey Who Rode in a Pocket, Keith Sparrow, artist

Chapter 14

Cruel Coppinger, Austin Robertson, Looe

The First Mole of Cornwall, Liz Berg, Liskeard

Thomasine Bonaventure, Esther Pinder, Launceston

SOURCES, FOLKLORISTS AND TELLERS

Arthur, Ross G. (translated by), *Three Arthurian Romances – Poems for Medieval France*. (Dent, 1996).

Baring-Gould, S., *A Book of Cornwall*, (Methuen, 1899).

Borlaise, William, *The Age of the Saints*, (Joseph Pollard, 1893).

Bray, Mrs Anna Elizabeth, *Peep at the Pixies, or Legends of the West* (1854).

Bray, Mrs Anna Elizabeth, *The Borders of the Tamar and the Tavy*, 3 Volumes, (W. Kent and Co., London, 1836).

Bottrell, W., *Traditions and Hearthside Stories of West Cornwall, Vol. 1*, originally contributed to the *Cornish Telegraph*, Penzance in 1860s and '70s, then reprinted in book form, (W. Cornish Penzance, 1870).

Camp, Mark and Birchward Harper, Barbara, *The Book of Looe*, (Halsgrove, 2008).

Causley, Charles, *Collected Poems 1951-1975*, (Papermac, Macmillan, 1983).

Couch, Johnathan, *The History of Polperro* (Dyllanstow Truran, 1969, 1871) .

Couch, M. and L. Quiller, *Ancient and Holy Wells of Cornwall* (1894, Tamara Publications, 1994).

Courtney, M.A., *Folklore – Legends of Cornwall*, (first pub. 1890, Cornwall Books, reprinted, 1989).

Courtney, M.A., *Cornish Folklore in the Folklore Journal, Vol. 5*, (1887).

Dawson, C.A., *Nooks and Corners of Cornwall*, (London, Eveleigh Nash).

Doble, G.H., *The Saints of Cornwall*, (The Holywell Press, Oxford, 1964).

Dunn, Mike, *The Looe Island Story*, (Polperro Heritage Press, 2005).

Harris, J. Henry, *Cornish Saints and Sinners*, (Oakmagic Pub. 1906).

Hawker, R.S., *Footprints of Former Men in Far Cornwall*, (John Lane, 1903).

Hunt, Robert, *Popular Romances of the West of England*, (London Chatto and Windus, 1881).

Moore, Peter and Lister, Martin, *The Good Looe Story*, (Peter Moore Publications, 1997).

Moore, Peter and Lister, Martin, *Liskeard Town and About*, (Tamara Publications, 1988).

Rawe, Donald R., ed., *Traditional Cornish Stories and Rhymes*, (Lodenick Press, 1992).

Rowe, Joseph Hamley, *Tristan, King Rivalen and King Mark*, (Truro, Oscar Blackford, 1928).

Spooner, Barbara, *Jan Tregagle of Trevovder: Man and Ghost*, (1935).

Tregarthen, Enys, *The House of the Sleeping Winds*, (London, Redman Ltd., 1911).

Tregarthen, Enys, *The Piskey Purse*, (London, Wells, Gardner, Darton & Co., Ltd., 1905).

Tregarthen, Enys, *Legends and Tales of North Cornwall*, (London, Wells Gardner, Darton & Co., Ltd., 1906).

Tregarthen, Enys, edited E. Yates, *Piskey Folk: A Book of Cornish Legends*, (John Day, 1942).

Tregidga, Garry, ed., *The Institute of Cornish Studies Book. 'Memory, Place and Identity'*, (Frances Boutle Publishers, 2012).

Unknown, *A Looe Ditty-Box*, (London and Scarborough, 1924).

Young, Simon, 'Her Room Was her World: Nellie Sloggett and North Cornish Folklore', *Journal of Ethnology and Folkloristics, volume 11*(2), (2017).

Traditional Tales from East Cornwall

www.mazedtales.org

Society *for*
Storytelling

Since 1993, The Society for Storytelling has championed the ancient art of oral storytelling and its long and honourable history – not just as entertainment, but also in education, health, and inspiring and changing lives. Storytellers, enthusiasts and academics support and are supported by this registered charity to ensure the art is nurtured and developed throughout the UK.

Many activities of the Society are available to all, such as locating storytellers on the Society website, taking part in our annual National Storytelling Week at the start of every February, purchasing our quarterly magazine Storylines, or attending our Annual Gathering – a chance to revel in engaging performances, inspiring workshops, and the company of like-minded people.

You can also become a member of the Society to support the work we do. In return, you receive free access to Storylines, discounted tickets to the Annual Gathering and other storytelling events, the opportunity to join our mentorship scheme for new storytellers, and more. Among our great deals for members is a 30% discount off titles from The History Press.

For more information, including how to join, please visit

www.sfs.org.uk

Printed in Great Britain
by Amazon